The West Virginia Book of Lists

The West Virginia Book of Lists

Gerald Tomlinson and Richard C. Weigen

BOOKS

Sutton, West Virginia

Copyright © 1994 by Gerald Tomlinson and Richard C. Weigen

All rights reserved. No part of this book may be reproduced, stored in a retrieval system, or transmitted in any form or by any means, electronic, mechanical, photocopying, recording, or otherwise, without written permission from the publisher.

Library of Congress Catalog Card Number: 94-076304   CIP

The information contained in this book is obtained from sources believed to be reliable. However, the authors make no representations or warranties with respect to the material listed herein and specifically disclaim any warranties with respect to the places named. Furthermore, inclusion in this book does not constitute a recommendation, nor does exclusion constitute a non-recommendation. Although every effort has been made to be as accurate as possible, the information herein is subject to change, and the authors make no representation that this book is free from error.

Mainstream America Books is an imprint of Home Run Press. For information, address Home Run Press, 19 Harbor Drive, Lake Hopatcong, NJ 07849.

If this book is not available at your local bookstore, you may order a copy by sending $15.00 to Strictly Business, Inc., P.O. Box 65, Sutton, WV 26601. West Virginia residents add 6% sales tax.

Cover photo: Pipestem Resort State Park, Larry Belcher,
               West Virginia Division of Tourism & Parks

Inside photos: Gerald Tomlinson

Printed in the United States of America

ISBN 0-917125-03-7

Preface

"Yes, Virginia, there is a West Virginia."

The Mountaineer State, the most irregularly shaped of all the fifty states, is also bedrock America, from the Eastern Gateway to the Metro Valley, from the Northern Panhandle to the New River/Greenbrier Valley.

It's a state of infinite variety.

This book shows in a concise, graphic way the many and varied reasons for West Virginia's pride: the people, the places, the events, the sights . . . and more. Our aim is to present in one small volume the state's most interesting talking points in a nutshell.

One point to remember: West Virginia was a part of Virginia until the Civil War. Before the Wheeling Conventions of 1863 (and statehood for what was then called Kanawha), West Virginia belonged part and parcel to the Old Dominion. Strictly speaking, then, Stonewall Jackson could not have been born in West Virginia. There was no West Virginia in 1824, the year of his birth. However, he was born in what today is West Virginia—and in this book, and in most modern histories, that is what decides.

So here you have it: West Virginia in 111 selected and, we hope, fascinating lists.

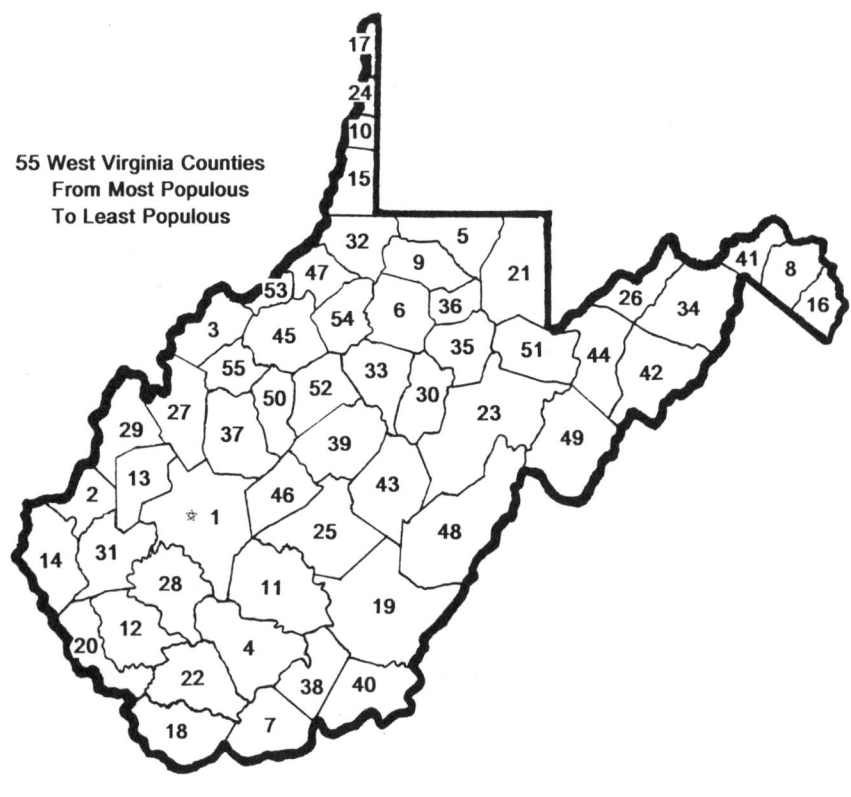

55 West Virginia Counties From Most Populous To Least Populous

1. Kanawha
2. Cabell
3. Wood
4. Raleigh
5. Monongalia
6. Harrison
7. Mercer
8. Berkeley
9. Marion
10. Ohio
11. Fayette
12. Logan
13. Putnam
14. Wayne
15. Marshall
16. Jefferson
17. Hancock
18. McDowell
19. Greenbrier
20. Mingo
21. Preston
22. Wyoming
23. Randolph
24. Brooke
25. Nicholas
26. Mineral
27. Jackson
28. Boone
29. Mason
30. Upshur
31. Lincoln
32. Wetzel
33. Lewis
34. Hampshire
35. Barbour
36. Taylor
37. Roane
38. Summers
39. Braxton
40. Monroe
41. Morgan
42. Hardy
43. Webster
44. Grant
45. Ritchie
46. Clay
47. Tyler
48. Pocahontas
49. Pendleton
50. Calhoun
51. Tucker
52. Gilmer
53. Pleasants
54. Doddridge
55. Wirt

Contents

People   13

  9 Famous Americans with Ties to West Virginia   14
  7 West Virginia Women Notable in U.S. History   15
  3 Native American (American Indian) Leaders
      Connected to What Is Now West Virginia   17
  4 Legendary West Virginians   18
  8 Civil War Generals Born in What Is Now
      West Virginia   20
  6 Country Music Stars Born in West Virginia   21
  3 Jazz Musicians from West Virginia   22
  3 Famous Opera Singers from West Virginia   23
  13 Outstanding West Virginia Craftspeople   23
  12 West Virginia-Born Actors and Actresses   25
  10 Well-known Novelists Born in West Virginia   27
  5 West Virginia Children's Book Authors   29
  4 West Virginia Mystery Writers   30
  6 Outstanding Athletes Born in West Virginia   32
  5 Famous Coaches Born in West Virginia   33
  10 Business Leaders from West Virginia   35
  3 Labor Leaders Born in West Virginia   37
  6 Bad-News Residents of West Virginia   39
  7 Well-known Politicians from West Virginia   41
  8 Cabinet Members with Ties to West Virginia   43
  32 West Virginia Governors   45

Places   49

55 West Virginia Counties
   (and Their County Seats)   50
5 Largest WV Counties by Land Area   52
5 West Virginia Counties Named for U.S. Presidents   53
3 West Virginia Counties Named for U.S. Senators   54
20 Largest Municipalities in West Virginia   55
12 Fastest Growing Towns in West Virginia   56
42 Communities in West Virginia Known (Only) on
   a First-Name Basis   57
16 West Virginia Place-Names That Contain
   the World "Coal"   58
42 West Virginia Communities with Three-Letter
   Names   59
15 West Virginia Towns with Unusual Names   60
19 Famous Foreign Cities in West Virginia   61
6 Towns in West Virginia Where the Weather
   Bears Watching   62
8 Towns in West Virginia Where All Is Well   62
3 West Virginia Communities That Have Been
   Called Charles Town   63
18 Towns in West Virginia Whose Names
   Have Changed . . . Often for the Better   64
7 Picturesque Towns in West Virginia   65
3 West Virginia Towns Built by the Federal
   Government   67
8 West Virginia Coal Towns   68
8 Faded West Virginia Boom Towns   69
6 West Virginia State Parks with Special
   Attractions   71
37 West Virginia State Parks   73
9 West Virginia State Forests   76

Events 77

    6 Civil War Battles Fought in West Virginia   78
    10 Worst Mine Disasters in West Virginia   80
    5 Famous but Unhappy Events in West Virginia   83
    10 Twentieth-Century Disasters in West Virginia
        (Other Than Mine Explosions)   84
    4 Labor Uprisings in West Virginia   86
    7 Highly Publicized Murder Cases in West Virginia
        Since 1969   87
    5 Major West Virginia Fairs and Festivals   89
    3 West Virginia Ramp Festivals   90
    5 Noteworthy Craft Fairs in West Virginia   91

Superlatives 93

    20 West Virginia Firsts   94
    10 West Virginia Superlatives   95
    9 Recreational Activities in Which West Virginia
        Ranks in the Top 10   97
    5 Things in Which West Virginia Ranks (Unhappily)
        Number One   97
    7 Things in Which West Virginia Stands Last
        Last in the Nation   98
    5 West Virginia Geophysical Superlatives   98
    7 West Virginia One-of-a-Kinds   99

Sights 101

    11 Major Rivers in West Virginia   102
    8 Rivers with Headwaters in Pocahontas County   102
    4 Spectacular Caves in West Virginia   103
    5 West Virginia Bridges of Some Renown   104
    5 Notable Covered Bridges in West Virginia   105

Sights (cont.)

10 West Virginia Lakes Created by Federal Dams	107
4 Endangered Plant Species in West Virginia	108
8 Endangered Wildlife Species in West Virginia	109
8 Historic West Virginia Houses	111
8 West Virginia Churches Worth a Special Visit	113
4 Distinguished Four-Year Colleges and Universities in West Virginia	115
5 Alternate-Use Buildings in West Virginia	116
7 Important West Virginia Museums	117

Businesses 119

10 Largest Private Employers in West Virginia	120
9 Famous Brand-Name Products Manufactured in West Virginia	120
11 Railroads in West Virginia	121
4 Once-Prosperous Industries in West Virginia	122
9 Companies with Large Land Holdings in West Virginia	123
12 Totals by Decade Showing Changes in West Virginia's Coal Industry	124
9 Notable West Virginia Glass Factories	125
4 Old Country Stores in West Virginia	126
10 West Virginia Bed & Breakfasts	128
7 Three-Star Restaurants in West Virginia	130
10 West Virginia Wineries	131
3 Places to Dine in West Virginia That Have Items Setting Them Apart	132
3 Early West Virginia Spas Still in Business	133
5 West Virginia Resorts of Yesteryear	134
5 Three-Star Resorts in West Virginia	136
7 Noteworthy Facts About The Greenbrier	137

CONTENTS • 11

Arts and Media 139

23 Daily Newspapers in West Virginia 140
4 Cities in West Virginia with Two Daily
    Newspapers 141
3 Official State Songs 141
4 Movies Filmed in West Virginia 142
5 Novels with West Virginia Settings 143
3 Short Story Collections That Feature
    West Virginia 144
4 Periodicals About West Virginia 145
6 West Virginia Professional Arts Groups 147
6 Active Regional and Community Arts Groups
    in West Virginia 148
4 Useful and Appealing Books About
    West Virginia 149

Sports 151

6 Baseball Hall-of-Famers Who Played
    Minor League Baseball in West Virginia 152
4 Places with Fewer Than 4,000 People
    That Once Had Professional Baseball 153
10 Major League Baseball Players Who Broke in
    with Bluefield 154
7 Pro Football Hall of Famers with Ties
    to West Virginia 156
5 Consensus Football All-Americans
    at West Virginia University 158
9 WVU Football Mountaineers Who Played
    in the Super Bowl 158
7 Basketball First-team All-Americans at WVU 159
11 WV High School Basketball Players with More
    Than 2,000 Career Points 161

Sports (cont.)

6 WV High School Football Players Who Scored 200 Points in a Season	161
9 Eye-Popping High School Sports Records	162
3 Great Rivers for Whitewater Rafting	164
6 West Virginia Ski Resorts	165
35 West Virginia Fishing Records	167

Sources   169

Index   173

About the Authors   192

People

This statue of Stonewall Jackson, Lee's ablest and most trusted general, stands in Clarksburg, where Jackson was born.

9 Famous Americans with Ties to West Virginia

There are many more than nine famous Americans with West Virginia connections. Most of the others are included on more specialized lists. With two exceptions, the men on this list achieved fame before West Virginia's statehood.

1. George Washington, 1732-1799 (Berkeley Springs *et al.*)
    As a soldier and surveyor, Washington spent a considerable amount of time in the late 1740s and 1750s in what is now West Virginia. He helped to popularize Berkeley Springs (then Bath) as a spa.

2. Daniel Boone, 1734-1820 [Kanawha]
    Born near present-day Reading, PA, frontiersman Boone is most often associated with Kentucky. But he lived for more than a decade in a log cabin on the Kanawha River near the mouth of Campbell's Creek.

3. James Rumsey, 1743-1792 (Shepherdstown)
    In 1787 Rumsey, a resident of Shepherdstown, exhibited a boat propelled by steam on the Potomac River. He was unable to raise the money to manufacture it.

4. Aaron Burr, 1756-1836 (near Parkersburg)
    Burr had killed Alexander Hamilton in a duel by the time he conspired with the Blennerhassetts of Blennerhassett Island in a separatist scheme for the West.

5. John Brown, 1800-1859 (Harpers Ferry, Charles Town)
    Brown was an abolitionist whose only connection with West Virginia was his raid on the federal armory at Harpers Ferry and his hanging at Charles Town.

6. Robert E. Lee, 1807-1870 (Harpers Ferry, Elkwater, *et al.*)
   A Virginian, Lee put down John Brown's insurrection. Two years later, the renowned general led Confederate forces unsuccessfully at the Battle of Cheat Mountain.

7. Thomas J. (Stonewall) Jackson, 1824-1863 (Clarksburg, Weston, Martinsburg, *et al.*)
   Stonewall Jackson, the brilliant Confederate general, was born and raised in what is now West Virginia. He grew up on his grandparents' farm near Weston.

8. Booker T. Washington, 1856-1915 (Malden)
   Born a slave, Washington worked in a coal mine before attending Hampton Institute. He taught in Malden and became principal of Tuskegee Institute in Alabama.

9. Charles (Chuck) Yeager, 1923- (Myra, Hamlin)
   On October 14, 1947, test pilot Chuck Yeager became the first person to break the sound barrier. A statue at Hamlin High School honors its famous graduate.

7 West Virginia Women Notable in U.S. History

1. Anne Royall, 1769-1854 (Sweet Springs)
   Born in Baltimore, Anne Newport was brought up in the home of William Royall, an eccentric farmer, who later married her. After his death, she became an indomitable crusading journalist and author, traveling all over the United States. President John Adams called her "a virago errant in enchanted armor."

2. Belle Boyd, 1844-1900 (Martinsburg)
    Actress and Confederate spy Belle Boyd was born in Martinsburg and lived there when the Civil War broke out. She provided Stonewall Jackson with valuable information about Union movements in the Shendandoah Valley. After the war she published an account of her activities, *Belle Boyd in Camp and Prison* (London, 1865), and lectured widely about her exploits.

3. Pearl S. Buck, 1892-1973 (Hillsboro)
    The Pulitzer and Nobel Prize winning novelist was born in her grandparents' house in Hillsboro while her missionary parents, on leave from China, were visiting. A brief stay as a baby is her only connection with West Virginia, but the Pearl S. Buck Birthplace Museum is a major tourist attraction.

4. Nancy Hanks, 1783?-1818 (Dolls Gap?)
    Notice those question marks. In 1967 Governor Hulett C. Smith set out to determine once and for all whether President Abraham Lincoln's mother was born in West Virginia. His search was exhaustive. The results were inconclusive. Nevertheless, a monument to her stands in Mineral County about three miles south of Antioch.

5. Nancy Hart, 1846-1902 (Summersville)
    In July 1861, Nancy Hart, then in her mid-teens, led a Confederate raid on Summersville. She captured a Union force and burned the town. Although seized in the fray, she used her charm and wiles on the man assigned to guard her, then killed him and escaped. After the war, she returned to Summersville.

6. Mary (Mother) Jones, 1830-1930 (statewide)
"If anyplace was home to Mother Jones, it was West Virginia. In five major strikes there, she wove herself into the social fabric of [the] state." So wrote Dale Fetherling in an admiring biography of the fearless and outspoken labor agitator. At the age of 91 Mother Jones harangued a crowd on the capitol grounds in Charleston, calling Governor Ephraim F. Morgan "a tool of the goddamned coal operators."

7. Betty Zane, 1766(?)-1831(?) (Wheeling)
Elizabeth (Betty) Zane was the sister of Ebenezer Zane, the founder of Wheeling, which was built on the site of Fort Henry. When the British besieged the fort in 1782—arguably the last battle of the Revolutionary War—Betty Zane ran 150 yards through gunfire to get needed powder. She brought it back to the fort in her apron. Zane Grey, a descendent, wrote a novel about the event.

3 Native American (American Indian) Leaders Connected to What Is Now West Virginia

1. Logan (Talgayeeta)
The great Mingo leader was an advocate for peace until April 1774 when a group of white settlers killed all but one of his family on the West Virginia side of the Ohio River. Logan's revenge and eloquent speech justifying it made him a famous figure.

2. Cornstalk (Colesquo)
    A great Shawnee war chief who led many raids against early West Virginia settlements, Cornstalk headed a force of about a thousand men at the Battle of Point Pleasant in 1774. Chief Cornstalk, who later became a voice for peace, was killed by white soldiers in 1777.

3. Blue Jacket (Marmaduke Van Swearingen)
    Born near present-day Richwood, this white-man-turned-Indian led 1,400 Shawnee warriors against Mad Anthony Wayne at the Battle of Fallen Timbers in 1794. The Indians were badly beaten in the encounter, which occurred southwest of present-day Toledo, OH.

4 Legendary West Virginians

There were two Mike Finks, both legendary. There may or may not have been a John Henry. There was definitely an Andrew S. Rowan (little known by name) and a Bricktop (known by the famous and infamous from Legs Diamond to Diana Ross).

1. Mike Fink, 1770?-1823? (Wheeling, *et al.*)
    This Mike Fink, an American frontier hero, was a keelboater on the Ohio and Mississippi Rivers. Known as the "Bully of the Boatmen," he was the Paul Bunyan, you might say, of the flatboats. In addition to his boating exploits, he excelled as a marksman, Indian fighter, and teller of tall tales. The *other* Mike Fink was a pioneer and hunter who roamed the Braxton-Calhoun County area and was killed by an Indian in 1780.

2. John Henry, late 1800s (Talcott, *et al.*)
   Whether the great steel-driving man actually existed is a matter of speculation. But he definitely lives in song and story. The powerful African American, thought to have been a freed slave from the South, reputedly raced a steam drill with a hammer in each hand (and won the race) while helping to build the Big Bend Tunnel of the C & O Railway. A striking statue of him stands near Route 3 in Talcott.

3. Andrew S. Rowan, 1857-1943 (Gap Mills)
   Who, you ask, is Andrew S. Rowan, and why is *he* a legend? Well, it was Rowan who "carried the message to Garcia." In May 1898 he was the first U.S. Army officer to enter Cuba after the outbreak of the Spanish-American war. Rowan carried vital information to General Garcia of the Cuban revolutionaries. Elbert Hubbard's 1,500-word essay, "A Message to Garcia," made the phrase (if not the message carrier) internationally famous.

4. Bricktop, 1894-1984 (Alderson)
   Her parents named her Ada Beatrice Queen Victoria Louise Virginia Smith, but it was as Bricktop that this scrappy, redheaded "colored girl" achieved fame in the 1920s and 1930s. Born in Alderson, she worked first as a saloon singer in Chicago before moving to Paris in 1924 and establishing a nightclub. A friend of countless celebrities, she later ran Bricktop's clubs in Biarritz, Mexico City, and Rome. Cole Porter composed "Miss Otis Regrets" for her to sing; Ernest Hemingway wrote about her; and T. S. Eliot put her in a poem.

8 Civil War Generals Born in What Is Now West Virginia

This list does not include brevet brigadier generals.

Confederate

1. Lt. Gen. Thomas J. (Stonewall) Jackson [Lewis]
    Jackson, the "strong right arm" of Lee, was mortally wounded at Chancellorsville in 1863.

2. Brig. Gen. Albert Gallatin Jenkins [Cabell]
    Twice wounded, he died at Cloyd's Mountain in 1864.

3. Brig. Gen. John McCausland [Mason]
    McCausland's troops burned Chambersburg, PA.

4. Brig. Gen. Birkett D. Fry [Kanawha]
    Wounded four times, he was captured at Gettysburg.

5. Brig. Gen. John Echols [Monroe]
    Echols led the Confederate forces at Droop Mountain.

Union

6. Maj. Gen. Jesse Reno [Ohio]
    Reno was killed at South Mountain, MD, in 1862.

7. Maj. Gen. Thomas M. Harris [Ritchie]
    A doctor before the war, he led troops in WV in 1864.

8. Brig. Gen. Isaac H. Duval [Brooke]
    Duval led the 1st Div., VIII Corps, at Opequon, 1864.

6 Country Music Stars Born in West Virginia

1. Red Sovine, 1918-1980 (Charleston)
    Perhaps best known for his deep-baritone dramatic recitations against an instrumental backdrop ("Phantom 309," "Teddy Bear"), Red Sovine was also a singer, guitarist, songwriter, and band leader.

2. Wilma Lee Cooper, 1921- (Valley Head)
    With her husband Stoney Cooper, Wilma Lee (Leary) Cooper sang traditional gospel songs and ballads as well as new songs, some written by one or both of them ("My Heart Keeps Crying," "Midnight Special").

3. Hawkshaw Hawkins, 1921-1963 (Huntington)
    Harold (Hawkshaw) Hawkins, "The Hawk of the West Virginia Hills," sang such songs as "Teardrops on Your Letter," "Slowpoke," and "I Wasted a Nickel." His biggest hit was "Lonesome 7-7203." He, Patsy Cline, and Cowboy Copas died in the crash of a private plane.

4. Little Jimmy Dickens, 1925- (Bolt)
    Standing 4'11"—"I'm Little but I'm Loud" was one of his hit songs—he had a distinctive twangy delivery that, like his subjects ("Take an Old Cold Tater," "Hillbilly Fever"), seemed outdated to many by the 1970s.

5. Charlie McCoy, 1941- (Oak Hill)
    A multi-talented performer, Charlie McCoy is famous mainly as a harmonica player in country music ("Today I Started Loving You Again," "Orange Blossom Special"), but he is also a fine guitarist and trumpeter.

6. Kathy Mattea, 19— (Cross Lanes)
"Unequalled among her generation of country singers," raved *People* magazine after the release of her second album, *From the Heart,* in 1985. Her first song atop the singles chart was "Love at the Five and Dime."

Country-Music Brothers from West Virginia

The four Bailes Brothers—Johnny, Walter, Homer, and Kyle—hailed from Charleston and began their professional careers in Huntington. Two of them were preachers, and "Dust on the Bible" was their most requested song.

The Lilly Brothers, Everett and Mitchell ("Bea"), gained their greatest fame at a honky tonk in Boston from 1952 to 1970. Born in Clear Creek, the Lilly Brothers helped to introduce Southern rural music to the Northeast.

---

3 Jazz Musicians from West Virginia

1. Don Redman, 1900-1964 (Piedmont)
    A saxophonist, composer, and arranger, Don Redman led his own band in the 1930s. Later he was a director for Pearl Bailey. Redman died in New York City.

2. Teddy Weatherford, 1903-1945 (Bluefield)
    Weatherford, a pianist, was a leading exponent of "Chicago-style" jazz in the 1920s. He died in India.

3. Leon ("Chu") Berry, 1910-1941 (Wheeling)
    Chu Berry was a tenor saxophonist with Cab Calloway from 1937 until his death in Conneaut, Ohio, in 1941.

3 Famous Opera Singers from West Virginia

1. Suzanne Fisher, 1903- (Flatwoods, Sutton)
    Educated in the Sutton public schools, Cincinnati Conservatory of Music, and Juilliard School of Music, soprano Suzanne Fisher debuted at the Met in 1935.

2. Eleanor Steber, 1916-1990 (Wheeling)
    Soprano Eleanor Steber made her debut at the Metropolitan Opera on December 7, 1940. She remained a leading soprano with the Met until 1963.

3. Phyllis Curtin, 1922- (Clarksburg)
    Phyllis Curtin, a soprano, first appeared with the New England Opera Theatre in Boston. She debuted with the New York City Opera in 1953 and the Met in 1961.

13 Outstanding West Virginia Craftspeople

West Virginia is home to hundreds of talented craftspeople. This list includes thirteen whose work is on display at The Cultural Center Shop in Charleston, a showcase for high quality handcrafts by West Virginia artists.

1. Joe Chasnoff (Lindside)
2. Judy Azulay (Lindside)
    These two accomplished woodworkers are partners in Chasnoff/Azulay. (304) 772-3580.
3. Joe Ehlerman (Bolivar/Harpers Ferry)
4. Karen Ehlerman (Bolivar / Harpers Ferry)
    The Ehlermans, owners of My Fathers Workshop, specialize in wooden toys and gifts. (304) 535-2549.

5. Jim Good (Gandeeville)
    As good as his name, this craftsman is one of the state's premier makers of dulcimers. (304) 577-6965.
6. Oral Henderson (Elkview)
    If it's a violin or a mandolin you want, Oral Henderson is the person to see. (304) 965-5925.
7. Ann Hickman (Sutton)
    West Virginia is noted for fine quilting, and so, especially, is Ann Hickman. (304) 765-5176.
8. David Houser (Moatsville)
    His business name, Houser's Stained Glass East, indicates the medium in which he excels. (304) 892-4372.
9. Keith Lahti (Floe)
    Beautiful clay pottery is Keith Lahti's specialty. It's called Floe Pottery. (304) 286-2635.
10. Connie McColley (Chloe)
    Tom McColley (Chloe)
    The McColleys, who call themselves Weavers of Wood, produce superb basketry and wood-turned objects. (304) 655-7429.
11. Chuck Matala (Morgantown)
    In his Wood Works workshop, Chuck Matala fashions handsome boxes and other items. (304) 291-6775.
12. Lou Ann Mohrman (Morgantown)
    Hand-braided and laced wool rugs and mats are her creations, under the name Braids. (304) 296-7501.
13. James R. Paden (Paden City)
    J. R. Paden works impressively in both wood and metal. (304) 337-8477.

12 West Virginia-Born Actors and Actresses

1. Henrietta Crosman, 1861-1944 (Wheeling)
   Primarily a stage actress, she made a few films, most notably *The Royal Family of Broadway* in 1930, which is available on video.

2. Dagmar [Virginia Ruth Egnor], 1920- (Huntington)
   She played a dumb blonde on the TV variety show *Broadway Open House* in 1950. Then in 1952 she starred in her own TV show, *Dagmar's Canteen*.

3. Joanne Dru, 1923- (Logan)
   Former model and a leading lady in films in the 1940s and '50s, she starred in *Abie's Irish Rose* (1946), *Red River* (1948), and *All the King's Men* (1949).

4. Don Knotts, 1924- (Morgantown)
   Probably best known as Barney Fife on TV's *The Andy Griffith Show*, comedian Knotts appeared in many movies and TV shows as a flighty but likable nitwit.

5. Peter Marshall, 1927- (Clarksburg)
   Not to be confused with the clerical "man called Peter," this TV personality hosted more than 5,000 shows of *The Hollywood Squares*.

6. Paul Dooley, 1928- (Parkersburg)
   Dooley, a character actor often associated with the films of director Robert Altman, appeared in Altman's *A Wedding* (1978) and John Cassavetes' *Big Trouble* (1985).

7. Tony Anthony, 1937- (Clarksburg)
    Tony Anthony starred in a number of spaghetti Westerns, among them *A Stranger in Town* (1967) and, with Ringo Starr, *Blindman* (1972).

8. Bernie Casey, 1940- (Wyco)
    Casey, a black supporting actor, appeared with former football great Jim Brown in two early bombs before moving up to better roles in *Cornbread, Earl and Me* (1975), and *Never Say Never Again* (1983).

9. Chris Sarandon, 1942- (Beckley)
    Character actor Chris Sarandon's best movie was probably *Dog Day Afternoon* (1975). He also starred as a sullen Jesus Christ in the TV movie *The Day Christ Died* (1980).

10. Conchata Ferrell, 1943- (Charleston)
    Fans of TV's *L.A. Law* will remember Ferrell as the brash, pudgy entertainment lawyer at McKenzie Brackman. Her finest film role was as a housekeeper for hard-bitten rancher Rip Torn in *Heartland* (1979).

11. Joyce DeWitt, 1949- (Wheeling)
    Television actress Joyce DeWitt played the part of Janet Wood in the popular TV series *Three's Company*.

12. Brad Dourif, 1950- (Huntington)
    A character actor, Brad Dourif made his film debut in the Oscar-winning *One Flew over the Cuckoo's Nest* (1975) and later had a role in the disastrous *Heaven's Gate* (1980). He has appeared in many recent films.

10 Well-known Novelists Born in West Virginia

1. Mary Lee Settle, 1918- (Charleston)
    Winner of the National Book Award in 1978 for *Blood Tie*, a story of expatriates living in Turkey, Mary Lee Settle is best known as a novelist, but she has also been acclaimed for her other writings, including the autobiographical *All the Brave Promises* (1966).

2. Davis Grubb, 1919-1980 (Moundsville)
    A novelist and short story writer, Grubb wrote about the lives of West Virginia mountain people. His first and best-known work, *The Night of the Hunter*, was made into a movie in 1955, starring Robert Mitchum.

3. William Hoffman, 1925- (Charleston)
    Hoffman's first novel, *The Trumpet Unblown*, was published in 1955. Several others followed, including *The Dark Mountains* (1963), and a collection of short stories, *Virginia Reels* (1979).

4. John Knowles, 1926- (Fairmont)
    A Separate Peace, Knowles's award-winnning first novel, was published in 1960. The setting is Devon, an Eastern prep school, similar to Phillips Exeter Academy, where Knowles studied.

5. Clyde Ware, 1932- (Clarksburg)
    Clyde Ware's career has been in motion pictures and television. The writer of countless TV scripts, he also produced two novels, *The Innocents* (1969) and *The Eden Tree* (1971).

6. Keith Maillard, 1942- (Wheeling)
    In the 1960s Maillard worked his way though the U.S. and Canada as a folksinger, photographer, music teacher, and writer. A Canadian citizen since 1976, much of his fiction, including his 1980 novel *Alex Driving South*, is set in West Virginia.

7. Meredith Sue Willis, 1946- (Clarksburg)
    A radical student activist in the late 1960s, Willis worked on three novels—the "Blair Morgan" trilogy—for more than a decade. Prior to that, she had published one novel, *A Space Apart*, in 1979.

8. Richard Currey, 1949- (Parkersburg)
    Fatal Light, Richard Currey's 1988 autobiographical novel, concerns a West Virginian who serves in Vietnam. Besides his novels, Currey has written poetry, short stories, novellas, and nonfiction.

9. Denise Giardina, 1951- (Bluefield)
    Denise Giardina, who calls herself "an Appalachian writer," is the author of *Storming Heaven*, a powerful novel about common people who rise to greatness at West Virginia's "Battle of Blair Mountain" in 1921.

10. Jayne Anne Phillips, 1952- (Buckhannon)
    One of the most gifted writers of her generation, Jayne Anne Phillips won many awards for her short stories before the appearance in 1984 of her novel *Machine Dreams*, praised by Nadine Gordimer as "an elegiac work [that] reaches one's deepest emotions."

5 West Virginia Children's Book Authors

There are more than five children's book authors with ties to West Virginia. Among the ones not shown below are Drollene Brown, Kate Buckley, Bonnie Collins, Marc Harshman, Colleen McKenna, Carole Marsh, Anna Smucker, Beverly Van Hook, and Becky Wilson-Kelly. But as these fine writers would readily admit, the following five are outstanding. Birthplaces are shown in roman type, WV connections in italics.

1. Jean Lee Latham, 1902- (Buckhannon)
    Beginning her career as head of the English department at Upshur County High School, Latham has since then written a dazzling array of juvenile fiction, nonfiction, and plays. She won the prestigious John Newbery Medal for *Carry On, Mr. Bowditch* in 1956.

2. Betsy Byars, 1928- *(Morgantown)*
    Born in Charlotte, NC, Betsy Byars wrote many of her highly acclaimed children's books in Morgantown, where her husband taught engineering at WVU. Her books portray lonely, vulnerable adolescents.

3. Nancy Evans Cooney, 1932 (Northfork)
    Nancy Evans Cooney taught junior high school in Northfork before moving away. She has written four children's books to date, the first of them *The Wobbly Tooth* in 1978. Cooney lives in Bridgewater, NJ.

4. Walter Dean Myers, 1937- (Martinsburg)
    One of the premier authors of fiction for young blacks, Myers has won a host of awards for his writing, includ-

ing the Coretta Scott King Award in 1980 for *The Young Landlords* and in 1984 for *Motown and Didi: A Love Story*. Myers lives in Jersey City, NJ.

5. Cynthia Rylant, 1957- *(Huntington)*
Born in Hopewell, VA, Rylant published her first book, *When I Was Young in the Mountains*, in 1982. It won a galaxy of awards, as did several of her later books. She attended colleges in West Virginia (Morris Harvey, Marshall) and taught at Marshall in 1979-80.

4 West Virginia Mystery Writers

The mystery genre is amorphous. Some 1950s critics viewed Davis Grubb's *The Night of the Hunter* as a mystery novel, while, more recently, Pinckney Benedict's *Dogs of God* has been reviewed in that category. In this book, however, those books and their authors are listed elsewhere.

1. Melville Davisson Post, 1869-1930 (Clarksburg)
Post, a lawyer and short story writer, won attention from serious literary critics for his detective tales featuring Uncle Abner (see page 142) and Randolph Mason. Critics of his day regarded Post as second only to Edgar Allan Poe as a short-story mystery writer.

2. John F. Suter, 1914- (Charleston)
A research chemist for 36 years, John F. Suter published "A Break in the Film," his first mystery short story in 1953. It earned a special prize in the *Ellery Queen's Mystery Magazine* of that year. Suter's later

Boley and McKee stories, such as "For a Coffin of Pine," are set in East Central West Virginia. Born in Lancaster, Pennsylvania, Suter has spent most of his life in West Virginia.

3. John Douglas, 1947-   (Berkeley Springs)

   Blind Spring Rambler (1988), John Douglas's second mystery novel is set in "Blind Spring," West Virginia, a company coal town that in 1923 is in the throes of a miners' strike. Youthful detective Bill Edmondson solves the case after his older partner is killed.

4. Carlene Thompson, 1952-   (Point Pleasant)

   Carlene Thompson's *Black for Remembrance* (1991) is a chilling psychological thriller about the apparent return of a mother's murdered five-year-old daughter after a 20-year hiatus. Her later novels are *All Fall Down* and *The Way You Look Tonight*.

Renowned mystery writer Melville Davisson Post wrote a long epitaph for himself that is inscribed on his grave marker in Clarksburg.

6 Outstanding Athletes Born in West Virginia

Since a whole section on sports appears later in the book (pages 151-68), this is just a preview. A few athletes missing from this list—some of them mentioned later—are shown below. Paul Popovich set high school records in basketball, but he played pro baseball. (Coaches have a list of their own, page 33.)

- *Baseball:* Lew Burdette (Nitro), Bill Mazeroski (Wheeling), Paul Popovich (Flemington), John Kruk (Charleston).
- *Basketball:* Hal Greer (Huntington), Rod Hundley (Charleston), Rod Thorn (Princeton)
- *Football:* Frank Gatski (Farmington), Gino Marchetti (Smithers), Curt Warner (Wyoming)

1. Jesse (The Crab) Burkett, 1870-1953 (Wheeling)
    For many decades, this little fellow, 5'8", 155 pounds, was the only West Virginia native to be inducted into the Baseball Hall of Fame. Burkett, an outfielder, hit .423 for the Cleveland Spiders in 1895, .410 in 1896.

2. Glenn Davis, 1934-   (Wellsburg)
    One of America's greatest track stars, Glenn Davis was a one-man team at Barberton, OH, High School. A star at Ohio State, he went on to win gold medals in the 1956 and 1960 Olympics for the 400-meter hurdles.

3. Sam Huff, 1934-   (Edna Gas)
    Coach George Allen picked Robert Lee (Sam) Huff, a 6'1", 230-pound linebacker, as one of pro football's 100 greatest players. After playing for Farmington High and WVU, Huff starred for the New York Giants.

4. Jerry West, 1938- (Cabin Creek)
   One of the great basketball players of all time, "Zeke from Cabin Creek" played for Charleston's East Bank High School, moved up to West Virginia University, and then starred as a pro for the Los Angeles Lakers.

5. George Brett, 1953- (Glen Dale)
   Brett, a third baseman who hit .390 for the Kansas City Royals in 1980, is a cinch to join Jesse Burkett in the Baseball Hall of Fame. Although born in West Virginia, Brett was brought up in California.

6. Mary Lou Retton, 1968- (Fairmont)
   "Sportswoman of 1984," Mary Lou Retton was the first American woman gymnast to win an individual medal in Olympic competition. She took a gold medal at the 1984 games in Los Angeles.

5 Famous Coaches Born in West Virginia

Football

1. Fielding Harris (Hurry Up) Yost, 1871-1946 (Fairview)
   The son of a general store owner, Yost graduated from Fairview High in 1889. After working in the oil fields, teaching school in Mineral County, and serving as a police chief, he starred for the Mountaineers (as a law school student) in 1895-96. His coaching fame stems from a 164-29-10 record with the Michigan Wolverines.

2. Earle (Greasy) Neale, 1891-1973 (Parkersburg)
   Neale starred in football, basketball, and baseball for West Virginia Wesleyan, 1912-14. After playing baseball for the Cincinnati Reds—with a World Series appearance against the Chicago "Black Sox" in 1919—he moved on to coach football for college and pro teams.

3. John McKay, 1923- (Everettsville)
   An All-State football running back and basketball guard at Shinnston High, McKay, the son of a coal mine superintendent, played at Oregon with quarterback Norm Van Brocklin. His greatest renown came as head football coach at the University of Southern California, where his Trojans won four national titles.

4. Louis (Lou) Holtz, 1937- (Follansbee)
   Holtz, a bus driver's son, graduated from high school in East Liverpool, OH. He played football at Kent State, then moved on to coach at various colleges. After a disappointing stint with the New York Jets in 1976, he returned to the college ranks, coaching Arkansas, Minnesota, and Notre Dame with great success.

Basketball

5. Clair Bee, 1900-1983 (Grafton)

   A graduate of Waynesburg College, Clair Bee gained prominence as head coach of the Long Island University Blackbirds, 1932-43 and 1946-51. His 410-86 record and .827 winning percentage are the best in college history. Bee, who coached the Baltimore Bullets in 1952-54, wrote many how-to and fictional books.

10 Business Leaders from West Virginia

Many of West Virginia's notable old-time businessmen, among them Henry Gassaway Davis and Stephen B. Elkins, achieved considerable fame in politics and thus are included on other lists. On this list, birthplaces are shown in regular type, West Virginia connections in italics.

1. William Gregg, 1800-1867 (near Carmichaels)
    Called the "father of the Southern textile industry," Gregg started out as a watchmaker in Columbia, SC. He later acquired a small cotton factory, moved to Charleston, SC, and in time built himself a company town, Graniteville, in the western part of the state.

2. Johnson N. Camden, 1828-1908 *(Parkersburg)*
    Born in Virginia, Camden rose to high positions in the petroleum and railroad industries in West Virginia. He organized the Camden Consolidated Oil Co., which later merged with Standard Oil. A Parkersburg bank president, he served as U.S. Senator from WV, 1881-87.

3. Michael Owens, 1859-1923 [Mason County]
    Owens learned the glass blower's trade at Wheeling and founded Union Flint Glass Co. in Martins Ferry, OH, in 1882. A few years later he began working for Libbey Glass Co. in Toledo, inventing many glass-making devices. Libbey ultimately became Libbey-Owens.

4. Ellsworth Statler, 1863-1928 *(Wheeling)*
    A Pennsylvania native, Statler grew up in Bridgeport, OH. At thirteen he became a bellboy in a Wheeling

hotel. Before long he was running a lunch room and billiard hall in Wheeling. He moved to Buffalo, NY, in 1896, where he opened the first of many Statler hotels.

5. Clarence W. Watson, 1864-1940 (Fairmont)
Engaged in coal mining from his early years, Watson formed several West Virginia coal companies which eventually were combined as Consolidation Coal Co. He served as U.S. Senator from WV, 1911-13, filling out the deceased Davis Elkins' unexpired term.

6. Michael Late Benedum, 1869-1959 (Bridgeport)
Known as "the great wildcatter," Benedum founded Benedum Trees Oil Co., an independent oil operation that developed new properties in the U.S., Mexico, and South America. The Benedum Trees office was in Pittsburgh.

7. Ernest Weir, 1875-1957 *(Clarksburg, Weirton)*
Born in Pittsburgh, Weir helped to organize the Phillips Sheet & Tin Plate Co. in Clarksburg in 1905. He became president in 1909, and in 1916 changed its name to the Weirton Steel Co. In 1929 he founded the National Steel Corp., making Weirton Steel a subsidiary of it.

8. Harry Sinclair, 1876-1956 (Wheeling)
After studying pharmacy at the University of Kansas, Sinclair found his true calling as an oil producer. He organized the Sinclair Oil and Refining Corporation in 1916. Involved in the Teapot Dome scandal of the Harding Administration, he served a prison term, but remained in charge at Sinclair.

9. Monroe J. Rathbone, 1900-1976 (Parkersburg)
 A chemical engineer, Rathbone rose through the ranks of Standard Oil Co., serving as president of the company, 1936-44, president of Esso, 1944-49, and director of Standard Oil, 1949-65.

10. William Batten, 1909- (Reedy)
 Initially in sales promotion for the Kellogg Co. of Battle Creek, MI, he moved to the J. C. Penney Co. in 1935 and advanced from assistant store manager to CEO, 1958-74, and board chairman, 1964-74. He was chairman of the New York Stock Exchange, 1976-84.

3 Labor Leaders Born in West Virginia

There have been many labor leaders from the Mountain State, and the three on this list achieved national prominence.

1. Walter Reuther, 1907-1970 (Wheeling)
 Reuther began as an apprentice tool and die maker at Wheeling Steel, later worked for GM and Ford, and became active in organizing the United Automobile Workers (UAW-CIO). He served as president of the CIO, 1952-55, and helped merge it with the AFL.

2. Arnold Ray Miller, 1923-1985 (Leewood)
 A bituminous coal miner for 25 years, Miller became president of the United Mine Workers of America in 1972, defeating the notorious W. A. (Tony) Boyle, who was seeking reelection. Miller held the office until 1979.

3. Sam Church, 1936 (Matewan)
    Samuel Morgan Church, Jr., succeeded Arnold Ray Miller as president of the UMWA, having served as the union's VP since 1977. A strike in 1981, a rejected first agreement, and a controversial second agreement brought mixed reactions. He lost the 1982 election.

Matewan, Sam Church's birthplace, was the site of labor violence in 1920. It gave its name and its story to a John Sayles' movie.

6 Bad-News Residents of West Virginia

Although West Virginia's crime rate in general is low compared to that of other states, the murder rate is a bit higher. This list names a few real hellhounds who have spent time in the state.

1. Thomas Boise (Parkersburg)
    Not long after West Virginia became a state, hard-drinking Thomas Boise, along with Daniel Grogan and another reveler, got into an argument with Abram Deem, a Wood County farmer, and shot him dead. Boise and Grogan were tried and sentenced to be hanged. Each argued loudly that the other should die first. The sheriff tried to hang them at the same time with a single rope, but it broke. When Grogan renewed his demand, the sheriff hanged him first, while Boise roared with laughter. A second noose quieted Boise.

2. John Wallace (Burton)
    In March 1878 John Wallace, alias John Baker, raped and murdered his sister-in-law, then dashed her infant child's brains out against a rail fence. Not satisfied, he returned to the cabin where the mother and daughter lived. He raped and murdered Ellen Church, a young woman who was temporarily working there. Lodged in the Black Hotel awaiting trial, he got swifter justice from a lynch mob. They snatched him from the hotel, took him to a nearby farm, and hanged him.

3. Harry F. Powers (Clarksburg)
    Pudgy, mild-mannered Harry F. Powers, a married man, wrote impassioned love letters to widows and divorcees, proposing marriage and inviting them to

Clarksburg. In a soundproof garage in neighboring Quiet Dell, he murdered two of them, one along with her three children. "Isn't that awful," he said when taken to view the bodies at the morgue. The jury thought so. He was hanged on March 18, 1932.

4. The Mad Butcher of West Virginia (Oak Hill)
    Between 1962 and 1964, seven men, most of them patrons of a local diner called the Four Minute Lunch, disappeared in or near the small mining community of Oak Hill. Only two carved-up bodies were ever positively identified, and the serial killer, who may or may not have been a West Virginian, was never caught

5. Charles Manson (McMechen)
    The man whose drug-crazed cult senselessly murdered actress Sharon Tate, heiress Abigail Folger, and half a dozen others near Los Angeles in 1969 was born in Cincinnati, OH, to an unwed mother from Ashland, KY. She deserted her baby, and Charles was brought up by his grandmother in McMechen. Soon shipped off to Boys Town, NE, he obviously resisted reform.

6. Sara Jane Moore (Charleston)
    On September 22, 1975, Sara Jane Moore, a matronly 45-year-old woman with a checkered background, tried to assassinate President Gerald R. Ford in San Francisco with a .30-caliber pistol she had bought the day before (her .44 having just been confiscated by police). Moore was born in Charleston, where she attended Stonewall Jackson High School, then drifted west to pursue an acting career, which did not materialize.

7 Well-known Politicians from West Virginia

The governors have all been politicians, of course, as have the members of the Presidents' cabinets. Both of those groups have lists of their own. This list contains seven prominent men with other noteworthy political achievements.

1. Henry Gassaway Davis, 1823-1916 (Piedmont, Elkins)
    Born in Baltimore, Henry G. Davis worked for the B&O Railroad in Piedmont and eventually became a railroad and coal magnate. He served as a U.S. Senator, 1871-83, and was the Democratic nominee for Vice President in 1904, running with Alton B. Parker against Theodore Roosevelt. Three towns in the state are named for him—Henry, Gassaway, and Davis.

2. W. H. Harvey, 1851-1936 (Buffalo)
    Okay, so Putnam County native William Hope Harvey, better known as "Coin" Harvey, held no political office. But as the author of *Coin's Financial School* (1894), the ex-Marshall College student had tremendous influence on the Populist Party and also on William Jennings Bryan, whose "Cross of Gold" speech in the Presidential election of 1896 embodied Coin's free-silver ideas.

3. Dwight Morrow, 1873-1931 (Huntington)
    A native of Huntington, Dwight Morrow studied law at Columbia and joined the New York law firm of Reed, Simpson, Thatcher and Barnum. A noted financier, he served as President Coolidge's Ambassador to Mexico and as a U.S. Senator from New Jersey. His daughter Anne married aviator Charles A. Lindbergh.

4. John W. Davis, 1873-1955 (Clarksburg)
    Davis taught law at Washington and Lee University before returning to his hometown of Clarksburg in 1897 to practice law. He was elected to the state legislature, then to Congress. After serving as Woodrow Wilson's Ambassador to Great Britain, he returned to the practice of law. The 1924 Democratic national convention chose him to run for President. He lost.

5. Harry Flood Byrd, 1887-1966 (Martinsburg)
    Harry Flood Byrd, like Dwight Morrow, is connected to West Virginia mainly through birth. He achieved prominence in Virginia as a newspaper publisher, agriculturalist, and Democratic politician. He became a state senator and then governor. From 1933 until his death in 1966 he was a U.S. Senator from Virginia.

6. Harley O. Staggers, Sr., 1907-1991 (Keyser)
    After teaching and coaching at Potomac State College in Keyser, Staggers, a Democrat, was elected sheriff of Mineral County in 1937. He moved up to the U.S. Congress in 1948 and represented the 2nd Congressional District until 1980, serving in the 81st through 96th Congresses. His son succeeded him in 1982.

7. Robert C. Byrd, 1917- (Stotesbury, Sophia)
    A self-made man who opened a grocery store in Sophia after World War II, Byrd progressed up the political ladder from the House of Delegates to the state senate to the U.S. House of Representatives, and, in 1958, the U.S. Senate, where he became Democratic Whip and later Majority Leader under President Jimmy Carter.

8 Cabinet Members with Ties to West Virginia

A number of U.S. Presidents have named West Virginia natives or residents to cabinet positions. A few served a substantial length of time; others were short-termers.

1. Nathan Goff, Jr., 1843-1920 (Clarksburg)
   A Union major at the end of the Civil War, Goff became a lawyer in Clarksburg. He twice ran for governor of West Virginia, was elected to both houses of Congress, and served as a U.S. circuit judge for many years. In 1881 President Rutherford B. Hayes appointed him Secretary of the Navy.

2. Stephen B. Elkins, 1841-1911 (Elkins)
   Born in Ohio, Elkins moved to West Virginia in 1890. He was Secretary of War, 1891-93, under President Benjamin Harrison. A U.S. Senator from West Virginia from 1895 to 1911, he was the author of the Elkins Act against the system of railroad rebates.

3. William L. Wilson, 1843-1900 (Morgantown)
   Born in Lexington, VA, William Lyne Wilson was president of WVU in 1882-83. He served in Congress, 1883-95, then became President Grover Cleveland's Postmaster General, 1895-97. At his death he was president of Washington and Lee University.

4. Newton D. Baker, 1871-1937 (Martinsburg)
   Born in Martinsburg, Baker was Secretary of War from 1916 to 1921 under President Woodrow Wilson. He practiced law and politics in Cleveland, Ohio, both

before and after his cabinet service. A pacifist, Baker was an outspoken advocate of the League of Nations.

5. Howard M. Gore, 1887-1947 (Clarksburg)
    Gore, born in Harrison County, graduated from West Virginia University. Primarily an agriculturalist and livestock breeder, he served as President Calvin Coolidge's Secretary of Agriculture, 1924-25, and then as governor of West Virginia, 1925-29. He held many high posts with agricultural organizations.

6. Louis A. Johnson, 1891-1966 (Clarksburg)
    A native of Roanoke, VA, Johnson practiced law in Clarksburg from 1912 and was active in Democratic politics. When James Forrestal committed suicide, President Harry S Truman named Johnson Secretary of Defense, a post he held in 1949-50.

7. Lewis L. Strauss, 1896-1974 (Charleston)
    Born in Charleston, Strauss was a financier with Kuhn, Loeb & Company, a rear admiral in World War II, and chairman of the Atomic Energy Commission, 1946-50. He served as President Dwight D. Eisenhower's unconfirmed choice as Secretary of Commerce in 1958-59.

8. Cyrus Vance, 1917- (Clarksburg)
    A corporate lawyer, partner in the New York City firm of Simpson Thatcher and Bartlett, Vance became President John F. Kennedy's Secretary of the Army, 1962-63 (not a cabinet-level position), and later served as President Jimmy Carter's Secretary of State, 1977-80.

32 West Virginia Governors

1. Arthur I. Boreman, 1823-1896
   Born: Waynesburg, PA   Republican: 1863-1869
2. Daniel D. T. Farnsworth, 1819-1892
   Born: Staten Island, NY   Republican: 1869-1869
3. William E. Stevenson, 1820-1883
   Born: Warren, PA   Republican: 1869-1871
4. John J. Jacob, 1829-1893
   Born: Romney   Democrat: 1871-1877
5. Henry M. Mathews, 1834-1884
   Born: Frankford   Democrat: 1877-1881
6. Jacob B. Jackson, 1829-1893
   Born: Parkersburg   Democrat: 1881-1885
7. Emanuel W. Wilson, 1844-1905
   Born: Harpers Ferry   Democrat: 1885-1890
8. A. Brooks Fleming, 1839-1923
   Born: Fairmont   Democrat: 1890-1893
9. William A. MacCorkle, 1857-1930
   Born: near Lexington, VA Democrat: 1893-1897
10. George W. Atkinson, 1845-1925
    Born: Kanawha County   Republican: 1897-1901
11. Albert B. White, 1856-1941
    Born: Cleveland, OH   Republican: 1901-1905
12. William M. O. Dawson, 1853-1916
    Born: Bloomington, MD   Republican: 1905-1909
13. William E. Glasscock, 1862-1925
    Born: Monongalia County Republican: 1909-1913

West Virginia's majestic Capitol, designed by Cass Gilbert and dedicated in 1932, is dominated by a 293-foot-high gilded dome.

14. Henry D. Hatfield, 1875-1962
    Born: Mate Creek   Republican: 1913-1917
15. John J. Cornwell, 1867-1954
    Born: Mole Hill   Democrat: 1917-1921
16. Ephraim F. Morgan, 1869-1949
    Born: near Forksburg   Republican: 1921-1925
17. Howard M. Gore, 1877-1947
    Born: Harrison County   Republican: 1925-1929
18. William G. Conley, 1866-1940
    Born: near Kingwood   Republican: 1929-1933
19. H. Guy Kump, 1877-1962
    Born: Capon Springs   Democrat: 1933-1937
20. Homer A. (Rocky) Holt, 1898-1976
    Born: Lewisburg   Democrat: 1937-1941
21. Matthew M. Neely, 1875-1958
    Born: near Grove   Democrat: 1941-1945
22. Clarence W. Meadows, 1904-1961
    Born: Beckley   Democrat: 1945-1949
23. Okey L. Patteson, 1898-
    Born: Dingess   Democrat: 1949-1953
24. William C. Marland, 1918-1965
    Born: Johnson City, IL   Democrat: 1953-1957
25. Cecil H. Underwood, 1922-
    Born: Josephs Mills   Republican: 1957-1961
26. W. W. Barron, 1911-
    Born: Elkins   Democrat: 1961-1965
27. Hulett C. Smith, 1918-
    Born: Beckley   Democrat: 1965-1969

28. Arch A. Moore, Jr., 1923-
    Born: Moundsville   Republican: 1969-1977
29. John D. (Jay) Rockefeller IV, 1937-
    Born: New York, NY   Democrat: 1977-1985
30. Arch A. Moore, Jr. (see #28)   Republican: 1985-1989
31. Gaston N. Caperton, 1940-
    Born: Charleston   Democrat: 1989-1997
32. Cecil H. Underwood, 1922-
    (see #25)   Republican: 1997-

The Youngest (and Oldest) Governor

Here are two trivia questions with the same answer. Who was the youngest governor of West Virginia? Who was the oldest? Right you are. When Cecil H. Underwood was elected governor in 1956, he was the youngest person in the history of the state to hold the office. By the time he was elected governor for the second time in 1996, he was the oldest person to win the office.

Places

Railroad tracks form the main street of Thurmond, an abandoned town on the New River that was once a major C&O shipping point.

55 West Virginia Counties (and Their County Seats)

The counties are listed in order of population, from the most populous [Kanawha] to the least populous [Wirt]. Figures are those of the official 1990 U.S. Census. Notice that Hancock and McDowell Counties had precisely the same number of people in this Census.

1. Kanawha County (Charleston) — 207,619
2. Cabell County (Huntington) — 96,827
3. Wood County (Parkersburg) — 86,915
4. Raleigh County (Beckley) — 76,819
5. Monongalia County (Morgantown) — 75,509
6. Harrison County (Clarksburg) — 69,371
7. Mercer County (Princeton) — 64,980
8. Berkeley County (Martinsburg) — 59,253
9. Marion County (Fairmont) — 57,249
10. Ohio County (Wheeling) — 50,871
11. Fayette County (Fayetteville) — 47,952
12. Logan County (Logan) — 43,032
13. Putnam County (Winfield) — 42,832
14. Wayne County (Wayne) — 41,636
15. Marshall County (Moundsville) — 37,356
16. Jefferson County (Charles Town) — 35,926
17. Hancock County (New Cumberland) — 35,233
18. McDowell County (Welch) — 35,233
19. Greenbrier County (Lewisburg) — 34,693

20. Mingo County (Williamson)	33,739
21. Preston County (Kingwood)	29,037
22. Wyoming County (Pineville)	28,990
23. Randolph County (Elkins)	27,803
24. Brooke County (Wellsburg)	26,992
25. Nicholas County (Summersville)	26,775
26. Mineral County (Keyser)	26,697
27. Jackson County (Ripley)	25,938
28. Boone County (Madison)	25,870
29. Mason County (Point Pleasant)	25,178
30. Upshur County (Buckhannon)	22,867
31. Lincoln County (Hamlin)	21,382
32. Wetzel County (New Martinsville)	19,258
33. Lewis County (Weston)	17,223
34. Hampshire County (Romney)	16,498
35. Barbour County (Philippi)	15,699
36. Taylor County (Grafton)	15,144
37. Roane County (Spencer)	15,120
38. Summers County (Hinton)	14,204
39. Braxton County (Sutton)	12,998
40. Monroe County (Union)	12,406
41. Morgan County (Berkeley Springs)	12,128
42. Hardy County (Moorefield)	10,977
43. Webster County (Webster Springs)	10,729
44. Grant County (Petersburg)	10,428
45. Ritchie County (Harrisville)	10,233

46. Clay County (Clay)	9,983
47. Tyler County (Middlebourne)	9,796
48. Pocahontas County (Marlinton)	9,008
49. Pendleton County (Franklin)	8,054
50. Calhoun County (Grantsville)	7,885
51. Tucker County (Parsons)	7,728
52. Gilmer County (Glenville)	7,669
53. Pleasants County (St. Marys)	7,546
54. Doddridge County (West Union)	6,994
55. Wirt County (Elizabeth)	5,192

5 Largest WV Counties by Land Area

1. Randolph County	1,040 square miles
2. Greenbrier County	1,025 square miles
3. Pocahontas County	942 square miles
4. Kanawha County	901 square miles
5. Pendleton County	698 square miles

And the Smallest . . .

Brooke County, between Hancock and Ohio Counties in the Northern Panhandle, contains just 92½ square miles. The only county in the state under 100 square miles, its county seat is Wellsburg.

5 West Virginia Counties Named for U.S. Presidents

Many of the counties in West Virginia are named after distinguished statesmen. In addition to the five Presidents on this list, there are counties honoring the three great Senators of the mid-nineteenth century—John C. Calhoun, Henry Clay, and Daniel Webster, page 54. Harrison County, by the way, was named for the father of our ninth President, and Tyler County was named for the father of our tenth President.

1. Jefferson County

    Formed from Berkeley County in 1801 and named for Thomas Jefferson, third President of the United States.

2. Monroe County

    Formed from Greenbrier County in 1799 and named for James Monroe, our fifth President.

3. Jackson County

    Formed from parts of Kanawha, Wood, and Mason Counties in 1831 and named for the seventh President, Andrew Jackson.

4. Lincoln County

    Formed in 1867 from parts of Kanawha, Cabell, Putnam, and Boone Counties and named for Abraham Lincoln, sixteenth President of the United States.

5. Grant County

    Formed from Hardy County in 1866 and named for General (soon to be President) Ulysses S. Grant.

3 West Virginia Counties Named for U.S. Senators

The great triumverate of pre-Civil War Senators—John C. Calhoun (South Carolina), Henry Clay (Kentucky), and Daniel Webster (Massachusetts)—are all honored by having had West Virginia counties named for them.

1. Calhoun County
    Created in 1856 from Gilmer County, its early county seats were located at Arnoldsville, Brooksville, and at the mouth of Pine Creek.

2. Clay County
    Formed in 1858 from parts of Braxton, Kanawha, and Nicholas counties, it is the home of the Golden Delicious apple, which originated on Porters Creek.

3. Webster County
    The last county in West Virginia to be formed before the separation from Virginia, it was created in 1860 from parts of Nicholas, Braxton, and Randolph counties.

Two Counties Named for Native Americans

Logan County, formed in 1824, is named for the great chief of the Mingos, profiled on page 17. Pocahontas County, established in 1821, takes its name from the Indian princess who supposedly saved John Smith from execution.

20 Largest Municipalities in West Virginia

Figures are from the official 1990 U.S. Census. Teays Valley, number 18 on the list, is unincorporated. [Counties are shown in brackets.]

1. Charleston [Kanawha] — 57,287
2. Huntington [Cabell] — 54,844
3. Wheeling [Ohio] — 34,882
4. Parkersburg [Wood] — 33,862
5. Morgantown [Monongalia] — 25,879
6. Weirton [Hancock] — 22,124
7. Fairmont [Marion] — 20,210
8. Beckley [Raleigh] — 18,296
9. Clarksburg [Harrison] — 18,059
10. Martinsburg [Berkeley] — 14,073
11. South Charleston [Kanawha] — 13,645
12. Bluefield [Mercer] — 12,756
13. St. Albans [Kanawha] — 11,192
14. Cross Lanes [Kanawha] — 10,878
15. Vienna [Wood] — 10,862
16. Moundsville [Marshall] — 10,753
17. Dunbar [Kanawha] — 8,697
18. Teays Valley [Putnam] — 8,436
19. Elkins [Randolph] — 7,420
20. Princeton [Mercer] — 7,043

12 Fastest Growing Towns in West Virginia

Although the population of the state as a whole dropped during the 1980s, some communities bucked the trend. Here are the places that posted the biggest gains, along with their percent of increase.

	1990 Census	1980 Census	+Pct.
1. Winfield	1,164	329	253.8
2. West Liberty	1,434	744	92.7
3. Bolivar	1,013	672	50.7
4. Beverly	696	475	46.5
5. Ellenboro	453	357	26.9
6. Quinwood	559	460	21.5
7. Hurricane	4,461	3,751	18.9
8. Lewisburg	3,598	3,065	17.4
9. Franklin	914	780	17.2
10. Ranson	2,890	2,471	17.0
11. Petersburg	2,360	2,084	13.2
12. Kingwood	3,243	2,877	12.7

And One Substantial Loser

A number of places in West Virginia are smaller now than they were in 1980. One of them is Bradshaw in McDowell County, which had 1,002 inhabitants in 1980 and only 394 in 1990, a percentage loss of 60.7.

42 Communities in West Virginia Known (Only) on a First-Name Basis

Place namers in the Mountaineer State seem to have a penchant for familiar given names. Three-letter names are included in the list on page 59. [Counties are shown in brackets.]

1. Alice [Gilmer]
2. Alma [Tyler]
3. Anthony [Greenbrier]
4. Arthur [Grant]
5. Beatrice [Ritchie]
6. Belle [Kanawha]
7. Beverly [Randolph]
8. Calvin [Nicholas]
9. Chloe [Calhoun]
10. Davy [McDowell]
11. Dorothy [Raleigh]
12. Eleanor [Putnam]
13. Elizabeth [Wirt]
14. Ethel [Logan]
15. Gary [McDowell]
16. Gilbert [Mingo]
17. Glen [Clay]
18. Grace [Roane]
19. Harvey [Fayette]
20. Henry [Grant]
21. Jesse [Wyoming]
22. Kermit [Mingo]
23. Leon [Mason]
24. Leroy [Jackson]
25. Lester [Raleigh]
26. Marie [Summers]
27. Martin [Grant]
28. Melissa [Cabell]
29. Milton [Cabell]
30. Myrtle [Mingo]
31. Neal [Wayne]
32. Omar [Logan]
33. Perry [Hardy]
34. Rita [Logan]
35. Rupert [Greenbrier]
36. Ruth [Kanawha]
37. Seth [Boone]
38. Sharon [Kanawha]
39. Shirley [Tyler]
40. Sylvester [Boone]
41. Thomas [Tucker]
42. Victor [Fayette]

16 West Virginia Place-Names That Include the Word "Coal"

1. Coalbottom [Boone]
2. Coalburg [Kanawha]
3. Coal City [Raleigh]
4. Coaldale [Mercer]
5. Coalfield [Fayette]
6. Coal Fork [Kanawha]
7. Coal Mountain [Wyoming]
8. Coalton [Randolph]
9. Coalwood [McDowell]
10. Forks-of-Coal [Kanawha]
11. Highcoal [Boone]
12. Hotcoal [Raleigh]
13. Montcoal [Raleigh]
14. Parcoal [Webster]
15. Secoal [Boone]
16. Stonecoal [Raleigh]

Coal cars stetch toward the horizon in Williamson, center of the "billion-dollar coal field."

42 West Virginia Communities With Three-Letter Names

A few places such as Keslers Cross Lanes and White Sulphur Springs have long names, but West Virginians seem to favor brevity. [Counties are shown in brackets.]

1. Ada [Mercer]
2. Bim [Boone]
3. Bud [Wyoming]
4. Dan [McDowell]
5. Don [Logan]
6. Duo [Greenbrier]
7. Eby [Taylor]
8. Elk [Tucker]
9. Eva [Ritchie]
10. Far [Wetzel]
11. Fry [Lincoln]
12. Gay [Jackson]
13. Gem [Braxton]
14. Hix [Summers]
15. Hoy [Hampshire]
16. Hur [Calhoun]
17. Ira [Clay]
18. Ivy [Upshur]
19. Job [Randolph]
20. Joy [Doddridge]
21. Man [Logan]
22. May [Pocahontas]
23. Mud [Lincoln]
24. Nat [Mason]
25. Odd [Raleigh]
26. Oka [Calhoun]
27. Ona [Cabell]
28. Orr [Preston]
29. Pad [Roane]
30. Pax [Fayette]
31. Pie [Mingo]
32. Poe [Nicholas]
33. Rig [Hardy]
34. Rio [Hampshire]
35. Six [McDowell]
36. Sod [Lincoln]
37. Sun [Fayette]
38. Tad [Kanawha]
39. Uno [Wyoming]
40. Ury [Raleigh]
41. Van [Boone]
42. War [McDowell]

15 West Virginia Towns with Unusual Names

These names are ones that don't fit on other lists, such as the list of towns with three-letter names (some of which are unusual) or the list of towns with weather-related names (all of which are unusual).

1. Big Isaac . . . in Doddridge County, southwest of Clarksburg
2. Crum . . . in Wayne County, near the Tug Fork of the Big Sandy River, northwest of Williamson
3. Cucumber . . . in McDowell County, south of Welch
4. Droop . . . in Pocahontas County, southwest of Marlinton
5. Gypsy . . . in Harrison County, north of Clarksburg
6. Left Hand . . . in Roane County, southeast of Spencer
7. Letter Gap . . . in Gilmer County, southwest of Glenville
8. Looneyville . . . in Roane County, southeast of Spencer (three miles from Left Hand)
9. New Era . . . in Jackson County, northeast of Ripley
10. Pickle Street . . . in Lewis County, west of Weston
11. Sam Black Church . . . in Greenbrier County, northwest of White Sulphur Springs
12. Tariff . . . in Roane County, southeast of Spencer
13. Twilight . . . in Boone County, northwest of Beckley
14. Uneeda . . . in Boone County, southeast of Madison
15. Wolf Pen . . . in Wyoming County, west of Pineville

19 Famous Foreign Cities in West Virginia

Since the United States is a nation of immigrants, every state has a host of places named after cities in the old country. Here are 19 of them in West Virginia. Each foreign country has been limited to one place name in the Mountain State, because some, particularly those in the United Kingdom, have a great many namesakes in the state. (Oh, yes, Burma is now Myanmar.)

1. Athens... Greece?... *No*, Mercer County
2. Berlin... Germany?... *No*, Lewis County
3. Cairo... Egypt?... *No*, Ritchie County
4. Calcutta... India?... *No*, Pleasants County
5. Geneva... Switzerland?... *No*, Roane County
6. Ghent... Belgium?... *No*, Raleigh County
7. Glasgow... Scotland?... *No*, Kanawha County
8. Killarney... Ireland?... *No*, Raleigh County
9. Lima... Peru?... *No*, Tyler County
10. London... England?... *No*, Kanawha County
11. Moscow... Russia?... *No*, Hancock County
12. Odessa... Ukraine?... *No*, Clay County
13. Ottawa... Canada?... *No*, Boone County
14. Palermo... Italy?... *No*, Lincoln County
15. Rangoon... Burma?... *No*, Barbour County
16. Santiago... Chile?... *No*, Taylor County
17. Shanghai... China?... *No*, Berkeley County
18. Vienna... Austria?... *No*, Wood County
19. Wellington... New Zealand?... *No*, Roane County

6 Towns in West Virginia Where the Weather Bears Watching

It might also pay to look over your shoulder occasionally in Volcano, Wood County, or to check the tomato plants in Frost, Pocahontas County.

1. Cyclone [Wyoming]
2. Hurricane [Putnam]
3. Mount Storm [Grant]
4. Skygusty [McDowell]
5. Tornado [Kanawha]
6. Windy [Wirt]

8 Towns in West Virginia Where All Is Well

1. Assurance [Monroe]
2. Comfort [Boone]
3. Confidence [Putnam]
4. Goodwill [Mercer]
5. Joy [Doddridge]
6. Justice [Mingo]
7. Prosperity [Raleigh]
8. Prudence [Fayette]

It **Is** the Mountain State

Given the terrain, it would be surprising if a good many towns besides Mount Storm weren't called "Mount" Something. No surprises. Among others, there are Mount Alto, Mount Carbon, Mount Clare, Mount Gay, Mount Hope, Mount Liberty, Mount Lookout, Mount Nebo, Mount Olive, Mount Tabor, Mount Vernon, and Mount Zion

3 West Virginia Communities That Have Been Called Charles Town

The problem often arose with the name *Newtown*. Settlers founding a new town naturally thought of calling it *Newtown* (there's one in Mingo County). Charles Town is more unusual.

1. Charleston [Kanawha]
    At first it was Fort Lee, although Richmond officials in the late 1700s tended to call it Clendenin's Settlement, or Clendenin's Station, after Colonel George Clendenin, who established the fort. In 1794 the community was named Charles Town for Clendenin's father, but users over the years shortened it to Charleston.

2. Wellsburg [Brooke]
    The present seat of Brooke County was chartered in 1790 and named Charles Town after Charles Prather, who bought the land from the original settlers and established a ferry service across the Ohio River. In 1816 residents, noting that there were too many Charles Towns, changed the name to Wellsburg in honor of Alexander Wells, Prather's son-in-law.

3. Charles Town [Jefferson]
    Around 1770 Colonel Charles Washington, George's youngest brother, acquired a large tract of land that included the site of the present town. When streets were laid out in 1786, the main steet was called Washington, and the other streets were given the Christian names of members of the Washington family. The town itself was named for the colonel.

18 Towns in West Virginia Whose Names Have Changed . . . Often for the Better

1. Anglin's Ford . . . is now Philippi
2. Cherry Tree Bottoms . . . is now Richwood
3. Clendenin's Settlement . . . is now Charleston
4. Cuppytown . . . is now New Cumberland
5. Flesherville . . . is now Weston
6. Fork Lick . . . is now Webster Springs
7. Fort Union . . . is now Lewisburg
8. Guyandotte . . . is now Huntington
9. Lunice Creek . . . is now Petersburg
10. Marlin's Bottom . . . is now Marlinton
11. Mecklenburg . . . is now Shepherdstown
12. Neal's Station . . . is now Parkersburg
13. Paddytown . . . is now Keyser
14. Pearsall's Flats . . . is now Romney
15. Pickens Bottom . . . is now St. Mary's
16. Tanners Cross Roads . . . is now Spencer
17. The Hole . . . is now Harpers Ferry
18. Ziggletown . . . is now Sistersville

A Mountain from a Mole Hill

Once upon a time, there was a community in Ritchie County named *Mole Hill*. The citizens, deciding a name change was in order, exercised a once-in-a-lifetime opportunity, changing their *Mole Hill* to a *Mountain*.

7 Picturesque Towns in West Virginia

This is a subjective list. There are many attractive small towns in the state. These seven are surely among them, whether or not they're the seven most picturesque.

1. Bramwell [Mercer]
    About ten miles northwest of Bluefield lies tiny Bramwell, home of eighteen or so millionaires at the turn of the century. Here, far from the dirt and noise of the coal mines, the wealthy built elegant homes, which can be seen on a self-guided walking or driving tour.

2. Union [Monroe]
    This tiny county seat, with a population of 566, is located in the hills south of Lewisburg on U.S. 219. A self-guided walking tour offers a glimpse into the past—dozens of nineteenth-century homes, Green Hill Cemetery, and the old courthouse and jail.

3. Lewisburg [Greenbrier]
    Located near White Sulphur Springs and The Greenbrier resort, Lewisburg is a Civil War town rich in history. Self-guided walking tours start at 105 Church Street, not far from the landmark Old Stone Presbyterian Church. Horse-drawn buggies are also available.

4. Helvetia [Randolph]
    Helvetia is a happy surprise. Who would expect to find a tiny Swiss hamlet lying in the beautiful, forested region south of Buckhannon? But it's there, a tiny community (it was once much larger) on the National Register of Historic Places. It's Switzerland in America.

5. Charles Town [Jefferson]

> On land which George Washington surveyed at age sixteen, his youngest brother Charles later established a town. Charles Town saw the hanging of John Brown and sustained heavy Civil War damage, but today it is a quiet place of restored mansions and period gardens.

6. Harpers Ferry [Jefferson]

> The spectacular setting of Harpers Ferry in the foothills of the Blue Ridge Mountains has been the scene of much history. John Brown's raid in 1859 was a prelude to the Civil War, during which the town changed hands eight times. The National Park Service has restored most of Harpers Ferry, and the town has become the state's most visited tourist attraction.

7. Shepherdstown [Jefferson]

> This picturesque town on the Potomac claims to be the oldest in West Virginia. It's certainly old, dating to the early 1730s. Shepherd College, founded in 1871, ranks as one of the state's best. A Shepherdstown walking tour includes the historic Entler Hotel, now a museum.

3 West Virginia Towns Built By the Federal Government

1. Nitro [Kanawha]
    In 1918 the U.S. government built Explosive Plant C on 1,800 acres of farm land to produce smokeless powder for the Allied forces. A thousand or so workers built the enormous plant—and also the city of Nitro, which became a bustling city of 35,000 almost overnight. After the war the plant was sold to a group of bankers who hoped to attact private industry to the idle factory buildings. It didn't work out. Many buildings were scrapped. Houses were sold to coal companies and shipped down the river. Today the city of Nitro is a major producer of chemicals.

2. Arthurdale [Preston]
    This community, southeast of Morgantown on Route 92, was one of three federal resettlement projects in West Virginia, established in President Franklin D. Roosevelt's first term. Each family received a house, a barn, and three acres of land. The houses were built of concrete blocks and were arranged in a semicircle. Eleanor Roosevelt often visited Arthurdale.

3. Eleanor [Putnam]
    Yes, the name comes from the Eleanor who was married to FDR. Located a few miles northwest of Nitro on Route 62, this town and nearby Red House Farms (at Red House) were Federal projects for homesteaders. So was Tygarts Valley Homesteads, southwest of Elkins, between Beverly and Mill Creek.

8 West Virginia Coal Towns

Eight? There are dozens of West Virginia coal towns, or coal camps. True, but if a Sunbelt visitor were to say, "Show me a coal town," you'd want to choose one with that old-time character. While there is no such thing as "typical," the following places have been recommended by one or more writers as exemplary.

1. Davy [McDowell]
2. Gary [McDowell]
3. Holden [Logan]
4. Itmann [Wyoming]
5. Tams [Raleigh]
6. Widen [Clay]
7. Wilcoe [McDowell]
8. Winding Gulf [Raleigh]

A statue of Logan, the great Mingo leader, stands near the Coal House in Williamson. Housing the Tug Valley Chamber of Commerce, the gleaming black building is constructed of coal blocks.

8 Faded West Virginia Boom Towns

Many West Virginia towns, particularly the coal towns on the New River in Fayette County, prospered for a while and then faded or died. Sometimes the place is now a ghost town—an abandoned town, completely deserted. But in several of the communities on this list there are still a few people on hand today.

1. Volcano [Wood]
    Volcano, whose lifeblood was petroleum, was a true boom town. It was built in the early 1870s and grew quickly to a population of almost 3,000—larger than Parkersbug at the time. On August 4, 1879, it burned and was abandoned.

2. Thurmond [Fayette]
    At the height of its boom days, Thurmond, a coal town, boasted a 100-room hotel, the Dun Glen, where a poker game went on nonstop, day and night (so it's said) for 13, 14, or 15 years (depending on the source). In 1910 Thurmond was the largest shipping point on the C&O.

3. Beury [Fayette]
    Beury, a few miles north of Thurmond, was home to the Simms & McNabb Brewery. As late as 1976 an elderly black woman—and no one else—lived in Beury. Her home was a cut-stone mansion in the once-bustling town.

4. Sewell [Fayette]
    In 1890 the New River community of Sewell had 500 people; today it is a ghost. When Jerry Taylor wrote

about Sewell in the January 1973 issue of *Wonderful West Virginia*, he described foundations and ruins of old stone buildings along the dusty, unused streets.

4. North Caperton [Fayette]
    Queen Victoria supposedly helped to establish North Caperton, which, like all the New River towns of the era, could be reached only via the C&O Railway.

5. Nuttalburg [Fayette]
    This coal town in the New River Gorge was owned by Henry Ford until 1929 or 1930. He visited it on occasion. Nuttalburg, which once had the largest tipple of its kind in the world, hugged the river for a mile.

6. Cass [Pocahontas]
    Once a booming lumber town, Cass today consists of ruins and a few restored buildings. It is the terminus of the Cass Scenic Railroad, which carries passengers to either Whittaker Station or Bald Knob and back.

7. Spruce [Pocahontas]
    The remains of another old lumbering town, Spruce is located at the headwaters of Leatherbark Creek and can be seen on the Bald Knob run of the Cass Scenic Railroad.

8. Arthurdale [Preston]
    This town was built by the federal government during Franklin D. Roosevelt's administration (see page 67). Eleanor Roosevelt visited Arthurdale occasionally during the 1930s, bringing it national publicity.

6 West Virginia State Parks With Special Attractions

All the state parks have something to recommend them, but the six on this list are particularly noteworthy for one or more attractions.

1. Berkeley Springs State Park (Berkeley Springs)
    On Washington Street in the center of town, this tiny seven-acre park features the warm-weather 1815 Roman Bath House and the year-round Main Bath House. The Roman Bath House has a small museum. On the grounds are a swimming pool and taps for free spring water. The town of Bath, as it was first called, was considered a "seat of sin" in pre-Civil War days.

2. Canaan Valley Resort State Park (Davis)
    A resort ski center for both downhill and cross-country skiing, Canaan Valley is located amid spectacular mountain scenery. It has a 250-room lodge, cabins, a restaurant and cafeteria, snow-making equipment, chairlifts, and ski rentals. Summertime features an 18-hole golf course, lighted tennis courts, and much more.

3. Cass Scenic Railroad State Park (Cass)
    Not far from Snowshoe ski resort and Green Bank National Radio Astronomy Observatory is Cass, a former lumbering town, now the terminus of eleven miles of restored railroad track leading to Bald Knob, the second highest point in the state. Powerful logging locomotives haul passengers in brightly colored cars converted from those used for logging.

4. Greenbrier River Trail (Caldwell to Cass, many entry points; Marlinton is the largest town on the trail)

   This is a hiking trail par excellence. Seventy-six miles long, it follows the old C&O Railroad bed and is nearly level the whole way. Scenery, fishing streams, and wildlife abound. The trail, like the railroad of old, crosses 35 bridges and goes through two tunnels.

5. Hawks Nest State Park (Ansted)

   Spectacular views from the stone lodge and a two-minute aerial tramway descent to the New River help make Hawks Nest one of the most popular of the state parks.

6. Pipestem Resort State Park (Pipestem)

   Pipestem is generally acclaimed as the gem of West Virginia's outstanding state park system. It has a host of attractions—magnificent scenery; two fine lodges, one reached only by an aerial tramway; golf courses; miniature golf; swimming pools; rental bicycles, riding horses, paddle boats, and more.

Wheeling's Great City Park

Oglebay Resort Park, three miles northeast of Wheeling, is a 1,500-acre municipal park that compares favorably with any of the superb state parks. It features a children's zoo, a natural science theater, a museum, an arboretum, swimming pools, golf courses, an impressive 204-room lodge, and a spectacular winter Festival of Lights. *Magnifique!*

37 West Virginia State Parks

The parks are listed in order of acreage, from the largest to the smallest. Mailing addresses and telephone numbers are shown. Reservations for lodges, cottages, cabins, and campsites often have to be made a year or so in advance.

1. Watoga   10,100 acres
    Star Rt. 1, Box 252, Marlinton, WV 24954   (304) 799-4087
2. Holly River   8,292 acres
    P.O. Box 70, Hacker Valley, WV 26222   (304) 493-6353
3. Cacapon Resort   6,115 acres
    Berkeley Springs, WV 25411   (304) 258-1022
4. Canaan Valley Resort   6,015 acres
    Rt. 1, Box 330, Davis, WV 26260   (304) 866-4121
5. Babcock   4,127 acres
    Rt. 1, Box 150, Clifftop, WV 25831   (304) 438-6205
6. Pipestem Resort   4,023 acres
    Box 150, Pipestem, WV 25979   (304) 466-1800
7. Beech Fork   3,981 acres
    Rt. 2, Box 333 Barboursville, WV 25504   (304) 522-0303
8. Stonewall Jackson Lake   3,800 acres
    Rt. 1, Roanoke, WV 26423   (304) 269-0523
9. Twin Falls Resort   3,776 acres
    P.O. Box 1023, Mullens, WV 25882   (304) 294-4000
10. Lost River   3,712 acres
    Rt. 2, Box 24, Mathias, WV 26812   (304) 897-5372
11. Chief Logan   3,303 acres
    Logan, WV 25601   (304) 792-7125
12. Cedar Creek   2,443 acres
    Rt. 1, Box 9, Glenville, WV 26351   (304) 462-7158

13. Bluestone   2,155 acres
       Rt. 3, Athens Star Rt., Hinton, WV 25951   (304) 466-1922
14. Tygart Lake   2,134 acres
       Rt. 1, Box 260, Grafton, WV 26354   (304) 265-2320
15. Blackwater Falls   1,688 acres
       Drawer 490, Davis, WV 26260   (304) 259-5216
16. North Bend   1,405 acres
       Cairo, WV 26337   (304) 643-2931
17. Tomlinson Run   1,398 acres
       P.O. Box 97, New Manchester, WV 26056   (304) 564-3651
18. Valley Falls   1,145 acres
       Rt. 6, Box 244, Fairmont, WV 26554   (304) 363-3319
19. Cass Scenic Railroad   1,089 acres
       Box 107, Cass, WV 24927   (304) 456-4300
20. Greenbrier River Trail   950 acres
       Star Rt. 1, Box 252, Marlinton, WV 24954   (304) 799-4087
21. Moncove Lake   896 acres
       P.O. Box 224, Gap Mills, WV 24941   (304) 772-3450
22. Little Beaver   562 acres
       Rt. 9, Box 179, Beaver, WV 25813   (304) 763-2494
23. Watters Smith Memorial   532 acres
       P.O. Box 296, Lost Creek, WV 26385   (304) 745-3081
24. Camp Creek   500+ acres
       Star Rt., Box 310, Camp Creek, WV 25820   (304) 425-9481
25. Blennerhassett Historical   500 acres
       P.O. Box 283, Parkersburg, WV 26102   (304) 428-3000
26. Pinnacle Rock   364 acres
       Box 342, Bramwell, WV 24715   (304) 248-8362
27. Audra   355 acres
       Rt. 4, Box 564, Buckhannon, WV 26201   (304) 457-1162

28. Droop Mountain Battlefield   287 acres
    H.C. 64, Box 189, Hillsboro, WV 24946   (304) 653-4254
29. Hawks Nest   276 acres
    P.O. Box 857, Ansted, WV 25812   (304) 658-5212
30. Pricketts Fort   188 acres
    Rt. 3, Box 403, Fairmont, WV (304) 363-3030
31. Carnifex Ferry Battlefield   156 acres
    Rt. 2, Box 435, Summersville, WV 26651   (304) 872-3773
32. Cathedral   132 acres
    Aurora, WV 26705   (304) 735-3771
33. Beartown   110 acres
    H.C. 64, Box 189, Hillsboro, WV 24946   (304) 653-4252
34. Grave Creek Mound   7.2 acres
    Box 527, Moundsville, WV 26041   (304) 843-1410
35. Berkeley Springs   7 acres
    Berkeley Springs, WV 25411   (304) 258-2711
36. Fairfax Stone Historic Monument   4 acres
    Davis, WV 26260   (304) 259-5216
37. Point Pleasant Battle Monument   4 acres
    No. 1 Main St., Point Pleasant, WV 25550   (304) 675-3330

Three National Rivers

In recent years three West Virginia rivers have been added to the National Park System. They are the New River Gorge National River, so designated in 1978. Then in 1988 the Gauley River National Recreation Area and the Bluestone Scenic National River were included.

9 West Virginia State Forests

The state forests are listed in order of acreage, from the largest to the smallest. Mailing addresses and telephone numbers are shown. As with the state parks, reservations for cabins and campsites often have to be made a year or so in advance.

1. Coopers Rock   12,713 acres
    Rt. 1, Box 270, Bruceton Mills, WV 26525   (304) 594-1561
2. Seneca   11,684 acres
    Rt. 1, Box 140, Dunmore, WV 24934   (304) 799-6213
3. Calvin Price   9,482 acres
    Star Rt. 1, Box 252, Marlinton, WV 24954   (304) 799-4087
4. Kumbrabow   9,474 acres
    P.O. Box 65, Huttonsville, WV 26273   (304) 335-2219
5. Kanawha   9,302 acres
    Rt. 2, Box 285, Charleston, WV 25314   (304) 346-5654
6. Cabwaylingo   8,123 acres
    Rt. 1, Dunlow, WV 25511   (304) 385-4255
7. Panther   7,810 acres
    Box 287, Panther, WV 24872   (304) 938-2252
8. Camp Creek   5,300+ acres
    Star Rt. 1, Box 310, Camp Creek, WV 25820   (304) 425-9481
9. Greenbrier   5,130 acres
    H.C. 30, Box 154, Caldwell, WV 24925   (304) 536-1944

Monongahela National Forest

This vast National Forest covers parts of nine counties in eastern West Virginia—Nicholas, Greenbrier, Webster, Randolph, Pocahontas, Tucker, Preston, Grant, Pendleton.

Events

The first land battle of the Civil War was fought near this two-lane covered bridge spanning the Tygart River at Philippi.

6 Civil War Battles Fought in West Virginia

1. Philippi, June 3, 1861

    About 1,500 Confederate troops, an advance element of Brig. Gen. Robert S. Garnett's force at Beverly, were conducting raids toward Grafton. They were routed by Union troops under Maj. Gen. George B. McClellan.

2. Rich Mountain, July 11, 1861

    Union Brig. Gen. William S. Rosecrans' troops defeated and cut off the escape route of a Confederate force under Lt. Col. John Pegram, who surrendered 553 officers and men.

3. Carrick's Ford, July 13, 1861

    After Pegram's defeat at Rich Mountain, Garnett's force retreated, slowed by rain, and fought a delaying action at Carrick's Ford on the Cheat River. At a nearby ford Garnett was killed in a rearguard action.

4. Carnifex Ferry, September 10, 1861

    Rosecrans' men attacked a strong Confederate position in the woods. The Confederates, under Brig. Gen. John B. Floyd, withdrew toward Dogwood Gap, although Union forces had suffered 150 casualties to Floyd's 20.

5. Cheat Mountain (Elkwater), September 10-15, 1861

    This was Robert E. Lee's first campaign of the Civil War. Facing a Union force under Brig. Gen. J. J. Reynolds, Lee was outmaneuvered and forced to retreat. Confederate casualties numbered 100. Reynolds reported 21 killed and wounded.

6. Droop Mountain, November 6, 1863

   The new state of West Virginia had been proclaimed in June 1863. A Union military victory would help to ensure its permanence. Brig. Gen. W. W. Averell's plan of attack worked perfectly, driving the Rebel troops under Brig. Gen. John Echols from the top of Droop Mountain.

Early Civil War engagements in West Virginia were minor actions with major consequences: They focused attention on Maj. Gen. George McClellan, the soon-to-be-promoted "Young Napoleon."

10 Worst Mine Disasters in West Virginia

These are arranged according to the number of fatalities. All but two of the disasters occurred prior to the 1930s. [Counties are shown in brackets.]

1. Monongah [Marion] December 6, 1907
    361 died. This was the worst mine disaster in U.S. history. The explosion, which occurred at 10:00 a.m., rocked two connected mines, No. 6 and No. 8, on opposite sides of the West Fork River.

2. Eccles [Raleigh] April 28, 1914
    181 died. Two connected mine shafts of the New River Collieries Company, owned by the Guggenheim family, were devastated by successive explosions and fire.

3. Benwood [Marshall] April 28, 1924
    119 died. The blast occurred at 7:20 a.m. A heavy rain fell throughout the day as bodies were removed from the Benwood mine of the Wheeling Steel Company.

4. Layland [Fayette] March 2, 1915
    112 died. So common were mine disasters in the early 1900s that the first report of this explosion in *The New York Times*, datelined Hinton, appeared on page 11.

5. Everettsville [Monongolia] April 30, 1927
    97 died. A terrific afternoon blast in the Everettsville mine of the New England Fuel and Transportation Company killed three men at the tipple outside the mine and 94 inside.

6. Bartley [McDowell] January 10, 1940
    91 died. Although mine safety had improved considerably by 1940, this explosion in Bartley No. 1 mine of the Pond Creek Pocahontas Coal Corporation ranks sixth on the list of West Virginia's most deadly.

7. Lochgelly [Fayette] January 29, 1907
    84 died. "There is no chance that any of the men will be taken out alive . . . ." That line from the news report of this disaster at the Stuart mine near Fayetteville was a sad litany of the time.

8. Jed [McDowell] March 26, 1912
    83 died. The doomed mine of the Jed Coal and Coke Company had been pronounced safe by an inspector only a few days before the explosion. "The families of the dead men are in sore straits," a reporter noted. "Work has been very slack at the mine." (The coal camp of Jed, six miles from Welch, no longer exists.)

9. Farmington [Marion] November 20, 1968
    78 died. By 1968 a mine disaster of this magnitude made the front page of *The New York Times*, with two photos and a map. The Consol No. 9 Mine, where the blast occurred, was less than ten miles from Monongah.

10. Switchback [McDowell] January 12, 1909
    67 died. Early reports frequently underestimated mine disaster fatalities, but at the Long Branch Colliery the first report, 105, was high. However, 51 men had died in a blast at the same mine two weeks earlier.

Now known as John Brown's Fort, this building was the fire-engine house of the Harpers Ferry Arsenal at the time of John Brown's raid in 1859. His men took refuge here when U.S. troops began arriving.

The scaffold is gone now, but this is the place in Charles Town where John Brown's quixotic but celebrated assault on slavery ended. He was hanged for treason seven weeks after his raid.

5 Famous but Unhappy Events in West Virginia

1. John Brown's seizing of federal armory and arsenal, 1859 (Harpers Ferry)
   Confidently expecting a slave uprising, John Brown led his quixotic attack on October 16, 1859. The government sent troops under Col. Robert E. Lee and Lt. J. E. B. Stuart. Brown was captured, tried, and executed.

2. Hanging of John Brown, 1859 (Charles Town)
   Brown proclaimed, "I did no wrong, but right." Some in the North agreed, but few in the South did. Driven to the scaffold on top of his coffin, Brown was hanged on December 2, less than two months after his raid.

3. Hatfield-McCoy feud, c.1880-c.1890 (near Williamson)
   The savage Tug Valley feud between the West Virginia family of "Devil Anse" Hatfield and the Kentucky family of "Old Ran'l" McCoy raged for a decade, with frightful atrocities, mostly against the McCoys.

4. Joe McCarthy's "205-Reds" speech, 1950 (Wheeling)
   Sen. McCarthy was talking to a small group of GOP party workers when he struck, almost casually, on the explosive campaign theme of Communists in government. He waved a paper that named them, he said. The ensuing furor ushered in "McCarthyism."

5. Death of Hank Williams at age 29, 1953 (Oak Hill)
   On New Year's Day the great country singer and composer died of heart failure in the back of his limousine as he was being driven to a concert in Marion, Ohio.

10 Twentieth-Century Disasters in West Virginia (Other Than Mine Explosions)

1. Ohio River flood, March 27-30, 1913
    Cities along the Ohio River and its main tributaries—including the cities of Wheeling, Parkersburg, Charleston, and Huntington—suffered some of their worst flooding ever. Thousands were left homeless.

2. Hawk's Nest Tunnel project, 1930-1933 (Gauley Bridge)
    As many as 700 workers died of silicosis after helping bore a tunnel to carry water from the New River to a Union Carbide power plant. The Hawk's Nest Tunnel was an engineering marvel but an industrial disaster.

3. Ohio River flood, January 26-27, 1937
    As bad as the 1913 flood was, the "super flood" of 1937 was termed "the greatest in the Ohio's history." *The New York Times* of January 27, 1937, estimated the homeless in West Virginia at 56,000, the dead at ten.

4. Tornado, June 23, 1944 (Shinnston *et al.*)
    The death toll from this twister far exceeded that of even the worst floods (prior to the Buffalo Creek disaster of 1972). Fifty people were estimated dead in West Virginia, with the heaviest loss of life in and near Shinnston, where at least 27 people died.

5. Crash of Air Force C-47 transport, April 8, 1951 (Charleston)
    Twenty-one Air National Guardsmen died when their twin-engine C-47 crashed attempting an instrument landing in fog and light rain at Kanawha Airport.

6. Silver Bridge collapse, December 15, 1967 (Point Pleasant)
    It was 5:00 p.m., and dozens of cars were on the 1,750-foot-long suspension bridge across the Ohio River between Point Pleasant and Kanauga, Ohio. The bridge gave way, sending 44 people to their deaths.

7. Southern Airways plane crash, November 14, 1970 (near Huntington)
    All 75 passengers perished in the crash of a chartered DC-9 from Kinston, North Carolina, as it approached Tri-State Airport at 7:40 p.m. in light rain and fog. Of these, 37 were Marshall University football players. The head football coach and his staff were also killed.

8. Buffalo Creek flood, February 26, 1972
    When a giant slag dam operated by the Buffalo Mining Company burst at 8:00 on a Sunday morning, a wall of black water thundered through the coal mining camps in Buffalo Creek Hollow, killing 125 people.

9. Willow Island scaffold collapse, April 27, 1978
    Scaffolding inside the cooling tower of an unfinished Ohio River power plant collapsed, plunging 51 workers 170 feet to their deaths. The U.S. government charged three companies with serious safety violations.

10. Hurricane Juan flood, November 1-5, 1985
    Eighteen inches of rain drenched parts of the Blue Ridge Mountains and sent the Monongahela, West Fork, Potomac, Greenbrier, and other rivers on a rampage. At least 40 people died in West Virginia.

4 Labor Uprisings in West Virginia

1. First nationwide labor strike, 1877 (Martinsburg)
    The strike began in Baltimore when forty employees of the B&O Railroad walked off their jobs in protest against wage cuts. They were immediately joined by 1,200 train workers in Martinsburg. The strike then spread quickly to other rail centers across the nation.

2. Statewide coal strike that won UMWA a foothold in the Kanawha field, 1902
    Despite mine owners' injunctions, evictions, strikebreakers, and yellow-dog contracts, the United Mine Workers of America won a nine-hour day for 7,000 miners, along with dues checkoffs, semimonthly paydays, and other concessions. Elderly pro-union agitator Mother Jones was on the scene for a while.

3. State's first and worst coal war, 1912-13 (Paint and Cabin Creeks)
    Mother Jones, at the age of 82, exhorted the miners. On Cabin Creek she held up the bloodstained coat of a wounded mine guard and told the crowd, "This is the first time I ever saw a goddamned mine guard's coat decorated to suit me."

4. Mingo and Logan County coal war, 1919-21
    This armed attempt to shut down the nonunion mines of Mingo and Logan Counties led to two notorious confrontations:

    ○ *Matewan Massacre,* May 19, 1920. Albert Felts, head of a detective agency, arrived in Matewan with eleven armed guards to evict union miners. Sheriff Sid Hatfield, a local folk hero, met him. Shooting erupted, and Felts was shot. He in turn gunned down the mayor of Matewan. Sharpshooting miners opened fire, killing seven detectives. Two union men also died in the fray.

o *Battle of Blair Mountain*, September 2-4, 1921. "General" Bill Blizzard, a youthful UMWA official, led 6,000 miners in a march on Logan. They were to cross Blair Mountain. Anti-union Sheriff Don Chafin of Logan assembled 3,000 defenders, reached the crest of the mountain first, and threw up breastworks. Mine operators hired aviators to run reconnaissance and bombing missions against the marchers. Six of their planes crashed, killing at least four aviators. Otherwise, casualties were low. The march was turned back.

7 Highly Publicized Murder Cases In West Virginia Since 1969

These eight cases all have the distinction (or perhaps it should be called the notoriety) of having received substantial coverage in *The New York Times*. A case that received even more attention, but is not included here because the victim recovered, was the January 2, 1970, car bombing that nearly killed Monongalia County Prosecutor Joseph Laurita, 32, in Morgantown.

1. Bailey Mass Murder, June 8, 1969 (Parkersburg)
    Susan Bailey, 15, and her brother, Roger, 13, siphoned gasoline from their father's truck, carried it in a wash-

tub to their one-story frame house, doused each of the six rooms with it, and set a fire. Killed in the blaze were their father, Charles Bailey, 41, his wife, Ruby, 36, and ten Bailey children, aged six months to 17 years.

2. Murder at Ada's Club, August 20, 1969 (Parkersburg)
    A former Marine, David L. Grimm, 25, went on a shooting spree that began at Ada's Club, a downtown nightspot, killing two people and wounding three. He tossed a gas grenade into the building and then began picking off patrons with a rifle as they fled.

3. Slaying of "Warden's Rat," March 20, 1973 (Moundsville)
    Prisoners held five guards hostage at the West Virginia Penitentiary after one inmate overpowered three guards, grabbed a set of keys, and released some fellow convicts. They murdered Willie Hale, whom they called "the warden's rat." The revolt ended at that point.

4. Fraternity Rite Slaying, October 20, 1974 (Bluefield)
    Being initiated into Tau Kappa Epsilon at Bluefield State College was no cakewalk. During the ceremony Michael Bishop, 20, of Lindside was mysteriously shot to death in a cabin in rural Pigeon Creek Hollow. The owner of the cabin was charged with murder.

5. Rainbow Family Murders, June 25, 1980 (near Marlinton)
    Two young women, ages 19 and 26, were hitchhiking to a counterculture gathering of the Rainbow Family in the Monongahela National Forest. They were shot to death in a field near Droop Mountain. Twelve years later, seven men, all living in Pocahontas County at the time, were charged with their murder.

6. Hare Krishna Murder, June 1983 (New Vrindaban)
Kirtanananda Swami Bhaktipada, founder of the New Vrindaban commune, received a 30-year sentence on June 20, 1991, for mail fraud and racketeering. One of the nine counts charged him with authorizing violence to maintain control over dissidents, including the murder of Charles St. Denis, a commune member.

7. Murder of Warren Duliere, April 30, 1992 (Capon Bridge)
Warren Duliere, 60, owner and sole reporter of the monthly *West Virginia Advocate*, was a crusading journalist who assailed the Ku Klux Klan, the sheriff's office, shoddy school construction, river pollution, and much more. Someone shot him to death in his garage with one of his own guns. Suicide was not ruled out.

5 Major West Virginia Fairs and Festivals

West Virginia has more than 160 annual fairs and festivals, so there is nearly always something to do and someplace to go in the Mountain State. The following five are among the largest and best known of these events.

1. State Fair of West Virginia (Lewisburg)
Mid-August. This fair, featuring agricultural events, nationally known entertainers, carnival rides, fireworks, and more, attracts 250,000-plus people each year. (304) 645-1090.

2. Sternwheel Regatta Festival (Charleston)
Late August. The *P. A. Denny*, Charleston's elegant sternwheeler, is one of the many attractions at this

week-long event. Also featured at the festival are parades, contests, a hot-air balloon race, and top entertainers. (304) 348-6419.

3. West Virginia Italian Heritage Festival (Clarksburg)
   Early September. This rollicking event of the Labor Day weekend offers Italian arts, music, contests, and entertainment. (304) 622-7314.

4. Mountain State Forest Festival (Elkins)
   Early October. The State Championship Fiddle and Banjo Contest is just one highlight of this week-long, fun-filled festival. Some of the events take place on the campus of Davis and Elkins College. (304) 636-1824.

5. Bridge Day (Fayetteville)
   Mid-October. The awesome New River Gorge Bridge on U.S. 19 is the site of this one-day event, on which the bridge is opened to pedestrians. Parachutists and bungee jumpers test their skill and nerve by leaping from the 876-foot-high span. (304) 465-5627.

3 West Virginia Ramp Festivals

Ramps are odoriferous wild leeks that some say taste like sweet green onions and others say taste (and smell) . . . well, awful. Be that as it may, in mid and late April, West Virginia ramps and ramp lovers are rampant.

1. Feast of the Ramson (Richwood)
   Mid April. Richwood calls itself the Ramp Capital of

the World, and the annual community feast has been a tradition for nearly six decades. (304) 846-6790.

2. International Ramp and Augusta Dulcimer Festival (Elkins)
    Late April. This festival combines the food and music of the Potomac Highlands into a single, memorable celebration. (304) 636-1903.

3. Clay County Ramp Dinner (Clay)
    Late April. The folks of Clay have been preparing, serving, and eating their pungent upland delicacy every spring for the past quarter century. (304) 587-4274.

5 Noteworthy Craft Fairs in West Virginia

Nearly every West Virginia fair and festival features crafts, or food, or both. Among the state's most notable craft fairs are these.

1. Rhododendron Art and Craft Festival (Charleston)
    Early June. This outdoor craft fair attracts artisans from thoughout the state, who display handmade glass, patchwork, painting, sculpture, and jewelry on the State Capitol grounds. (304) 744-4323.

2. Mountain Heritage Arts & Crafts Festival (Charles Town)
    Early June. One of the most prestigious festivals on the East Coast, this springtime event (see #5 below) attracts some 200 craftspersons noted for the high quality of their projects. (800) 624-0577 or (304) 725-2055.

3. Mountain State Art and Craft Fair (Ripley)
    Late June, early July. Held at Cedar Lakes, this craft fair is the state's largest. For more than 30 years the juried show has provided a showcase for authentic, traditional Appalachian art and craft work. More than 200 craftspeople and special exhibitors display and sell their products. (304) 372-7860.

4. Stonewall Jackson Heritage Art and Craft Jubilee (Jackson's Mill, near Weston)
    Early September. The Jubilee features more than 140 craftspeople selling and demonstrating their handmade wares. In addition, there are historical reenactments, contests, shows, concerts, and home-cooked foods. (800) 296-1863 or (304) 269-1863.

5. Fall Mountain Heritage Arts & Crafts Festival (Charles Town)
    Late September. Sponsored by the Jefferson County Chamber of Commerce, this is Charles Town's fall gathering of craftspeople (see #2 above). It has been held annually for the past two decades. (800) 624-0577 or (304) 725-2055.

Superlatives

The National Radio Astronomy Observatory, Green Bank, has several impressive telescopes. A gigantic new one is being built.

20 West Virginia Firsts

1. First public spa in U.S. opened, 1756 (Berkeley Springs, which in those days was Bath, Virginia)
2. First battle of Revolutionary War fought (or was it the last battle of the French and Indian War?), October 10, 1774 (Point Pleasant)
3. First steamboat, invented by James Rumsey, launched, December 3, 1787, on Potomac River (Shepherdstown)
4. First U.S. trust (combination in restraint of trade) created by merging salt wells, November 10, 1817 (Kanawha Valley)
5. First newspaper to appeal primarily to women, the *Ladies Garland*, published, February 14, 1824 (Harpers Ferry)
6. First Methodist Protestant Church in U.S. organized at Old Harmony Church, 1829 (near Jane Lew)
7. First patent for a soda fountain granted to George Dulty, 1833 (Wheeling)
8. First Union soldier killed in Civil War, T. Bailey Brown, died May 22, 1861 (Fetterman section of Grafton)
9. First land battle of Civil War fought, June 3, 1861 (Philippi)
10. First street in the world to be paved with bricks, Summers Street between Kanawha and Virginia Streets, October 3, 1870 (Charleston)
11. First nationwide strike began when B&O Railroad workers walked off the job, 1877 (Martinsburg)
12. First rural free delivery of mail began, October 6, 1896 (Charles Town)

13. First Mother's Day celebrated, May 10, 1908 (Grafton)
14. First Golden Delicious apple produced, 1912 [Clay]
15. First organized 4-H Camp in the world held, 1915 [Randolph]
16. First state sales tax in U.S. imposed, July 1, 1921
17. First gasoline tax in U.S. imposed, 1923
18. First faster-than-sound flight made by Charles (Chuck) Yeager of Hamlin, October 14, 1947
19. First tunnel monitored by television, the West Virginia Memorial Tunnel, opened, November 8, 1954
20. First court in U.S. to admit videotaped evidence, convicting a drunk driver, Municipal Court, 1967 (Charleston)

10 West Virginia Superlatives

1. Largest Native American burial mound in U.S. (Moundsville)
    In Grave Creek Mound State Park, this prehistoric burial mound—79 feet high, 900 feet around, and 50 feet across the top—was first opened on March 9, 1838.

2. Oldest white oak on record (Mingo)
    Estimated to be 582 years old, the Mingo Oak, the largest and oldest white oak tree on record, was declared dead and was felled on September 10, 1938.

3. World's largest sycamore tree (Webster Springs)
    This tree is located on the Back Fork of the Elk River.

4. World's greatest gas well   [Tyler]
    "Big Moses," producing 100,000,000 cubic feet of gas per day, was drilled in 1894.

5. Largest alluvial diamond in North America   (Peterstown)
    In April 1928 Grover Jones and his son "Punch" found a 34.46 metric-carat diamond, the largest ever in North America, while pitching horseshoes in a vacant lot.

6. World's longest steel arch bridge   (near Fayetteville)
    On U.S. Route 19, rising 876 feet above the New River Gorge National River, is this four-lane, single-arch, single-span engineering marvel. It is 3,030 feet long.

7. World's largest axe factory   (Charleston)
    This factory no longest exists. When it did, it took up 50 acres and produced 48,000 implements a day.

8. World's largest clothespin factory   (Richwood)
    Once all those trees were cut down with axes from Charleston, they had to be made into something. How about clothespins? At Richwood was the first and biggest clothespin factory on earth.

9. World's largest railroad flatbed car   (Port Amherst)
    Amherst Industries built this behemoth in 1970—125 feet long, 12 feet wide, with a capacity of 150,000 tons.

10. Longest freight train on record   (Iager)
    This train, approximately four miles long, consisted of 500 coal cars pulled by three 3,600-h.p. diesels, with three more diesels 300 cars back. Weighing more than 47,000 tons, it traveled 157 miles to Portsmouth, Ohio.

9 Recreational Activities in Which West Virginia Ranks in the Top 10

West Virginia has an outstanding state park system, ranking seventh in the number of state parks and recreation areas per capita and fourth in state revenues derived from them. Not surprisingly, West Virginians are active in outdoor pastimes. Per capita participation in each of the following sports and exercises is among the highest in the nation. The number after each activity indicates West Virginia's standing among the fifty states and the District of Columbia.

1. Hunting - 3
2. Swimming - 4
3. Tennis - 4
4. Golf - 5
5. Camping - 6
6. Baseball - 6
7. Exercise walking - 6
8. Bowling - 8
9. Bicycle riding - 9

5 Things in Which West Virginia Ranks (Unhappily) Number One

The *Congressional Quarterly* is a gold mine—or, in this case, a toxic landfill—of comparative statistics. In a list of 325 West Virginia standings in fields ranging from agriculture to business to health to transportation, the Mountain State emerges at the top in only these five areas.

1. Sales of existing homes
2. Teenage unemployment
3. Deaths from heart disease
4. Prevalence of smoking
5. Deaths due to diabetes

7 Things in Which West Virginia Stands Last in the Nation

In the *Congressional Quarterly* the District of Columbia is counted as a state. Consequently, to rank last in the nation is to be fifty-first. That's where West Virginia stands in the following seven categories. The rankings are based on per-capita figures.

1. Retail sales
2. Total crimes
3. Liquor consumption
4. Births
5. Hispanic population
6. Asian-American population
7. Native American (American Indian) population

5 West Virginia Geophysical Superlatives

West Virginia is the most irregularly shaped of all the states—which, in itself, is a superlative. Here are five more.

1. Highest point in state: Spruce Knob [Pendleton], 4,861 feet
2. Lowest point in state: Harpers Ferry [Jefferson], 240 feet
3. Highest recorded temperature: 112° F., Martinsburg, July 10, 1936
4. Lowest recorded temperature: -37° F., Lewisburg, December 30, 1917
5. Highest county east of Mississippi River: Pocahontas

7 West Virginia One-of-a-Kinds

This list includes one-of-kinds for West Virginia (such as Camden Park) and one-of-a-kinds for the whole nation (such as the Federal Prison Camp at Alderson).

1. Good Children's Zoo (Wheeling)
    The only accredited zoo in the state, this 65-acre facility is a part of the Oglebay Resort Park. Its collection consists of North American animals in their natural habitat—deer, bison, black bear, otters, red wolves. The Children's Farm section has domesticated animals that can be fed and petted.

2. Camden Park (Huntington)
    West Virginia's only amusement park offers 28 rides, including the Big Dipper roller coaster, the Thunderbolt Express to Splashdown, and, for the less venturesome, a merry-go-round or a one-hour Ohio River cruise on the *C. P. Huntington*, a 77-foot sternwheeler that is docked at the park.

3. State Capitol (Charleston)
    Clearly, the state can have only one State Capitol, and West Virginia's is something special. Designed by noted architect Cass Gilbert, it is the last monumental capitol of Renaissance design built in the United States. Its gold-leaf dome is five feet higher than the U.S. Capitol's. A magnificent chandelier hangs in the rotunda.

4. Federal Prison Camp (Alderson)
    Established as a reformatory for women in 1927, this is the only federal prison facility in the United States that

is exclusively for women. In the late 1970s, when it had a maximum security unit, it housed, among others, Assata Shakur (Joanne Chesimard), the black militant who murdered a state trooper on the New Jersey Turnpike in 1973.

5. The Greenbrier (White Sulphur Springs)
Although West Virginia has several fine resorts, only The Greenbrier gets a Five-Star rating in the *Mobil Travel Guide* and a Five-Diamond rating from the American Automobile Association (see page 137).

6. National Radio Astronomy Observatory (Green Bank)
The NRAO, located in Deer Creek Valley about 35 miles northeast of Marlinton, has six radio telescopes and a seventh under construction. One of them is the world's largest equatorially mounted telescope. Another, nearly completed, will be the world's largest fully steerable radio scope.

7. Personal Rapid Transit (Morgantown)
Opened in 1975, the PRT is a fully automated mini-train system that whisks students from place to place on West Virginia University's three campuses. A $120 million demonstration project of West Virginia's Department of Transportation and the university, it provides free transportation to students, charging others fifty cents.

Sights

Breathtaking mountain scenery is almost commonplace in the Mountain State. This vista is at Coopers Rock State Forest.

11 Major Rivers in West Virginia

These rivers are either within the state or border it. The miles shown are within or bordering West Virginia.

1. Ohio	277 miles
2. Potomac	112 miles
South Branch	133 miles
North Branch	97 miles
3. Monongahela	37 miles
Cheat	159 miles
West Fork	102 miles
Tygart Valley	133 miles
4. Kanawha	97 miles
Coal	70 miles
5. New	87 miles
6. Big Sandy	27 miles
Tug Fork	55 miles
7. Greenbrier	167 miles
8. Gauley	105 miles
9. Elk	172 miles
10. Guyandotte	166 miles
11. Little Kanawha	167 miles

8 Rivers with Headwaters In Pocahontas County

1. Greenbrier
2. Cherry
3. Elk
4. Cheat
5. Gauley
6. Tygart Valley
7. Williams
8. Cranbury

4 Spectacular Caves in West Virginia

1. Organ Cave (Ronceverte)
    The largest limestone formation in this cave resembles a huge church organ. Discovered in 1704, Organ Cave was used for religious services by 1,100 of Lee's Confederate soldiers during the Civil War. They also used it as a source of saltpetre, an ingredient of gunpowder. Thirty-seven wooden saltpetre hoppers remain.

2. Lost World Caverns (Lewisburg)
    In addition to the regular walking tours of Lost World Caverns, the management offers "Wild Cave Adventures," three- to four-hour trips with expert cave guides into the noncommercial sections of Lost World and some of the other 1,500 local caves.

3. Seneca Caverns (Riverton)
    West Virginia's largest caverns, lying anywhere from 25 feet to 165 feet below the surface, are located in the Germany Valley section of Pendleton County. A variety of beautiful formations can be seen on the 35-minute walking tour, including "Mirror Lake," the "Grand Ballroom," and "Candy Mountain."

4. Smoke Hole Caverns (Seneca Rocks)
    The Seneca Indians used the front section of Smoke Hole Caverns to smoke and preserve venison and other wild game. During the Civil War, both sides used the caverns to store ammunition. Moonshiners later produced corn whiskey here, and an abandoned still has been preserved for display. The caverns, open year-round, are among the state's most magnificent.

5 West Virginia Bridges of Some Renown

West Virginia's covered bridges have a list of their own.

1. Wheeling Suspension Bridge over the Ohio River
    The first bridge built over the Ohio, this was the first suspension bridge of its kind in the world (and the longest for many years). It was built in 1849. Today it is the oldest suspension bridge still in use.

2. Silver Bridge over the Ohio River at Point Pleasant
    This unusual chain-link suspension bridge was one of only three in the world with this design, two of them in the West Virginia). It fell into the river in 1967. Shortly thereafter, the other one—at St. Marys—was destroyed.

3. East Huntington Bridge over the Ohio River
    One of the newer spans over the Ohio, this bridge is an engineering first, having a single concrete tower to support its cable-stayed box-girder design. An even newer bridge of the same kind spans the Ohio at Weirton.

4. Huntley-Brinkley Bridge near Wayne
    On Route 152 (formerly Route 52) this was a one-lane bridge at the time of the West Virginia Democratic primary in 1960. Newcasters Chet Huntley and David Brinkley mentioned it on national television. *Voila!* It was replaced, and the new bridge named for them.

5. New River Gorge Bridge near Fayetteville
    This spectacular span, with a magnificent view, is on U.S. Route 191 on Corridor "L." It is the longest and second highest single-arch steel bridge in the world.

5 Notable Covered Bridges in West Virginia

What was the point in building roofs on bridges in the first place? To keep snow off the roadway? To protect travelers from the elements? Not really. Bridges were covered to protect the elaborate hand-hewn wooden truss system that supported them. With the advent of concrete and steel, covered bridges were no longer practical. Even so, there were nearly 90 of them left in the state in the late 1940s. Today there are only 17. All are worth seeing, but the following five have special points of interest.

1. Philippi Covered Bridge

    On Route 250 in Philippi, this bridge, 285 feet, 10 inches long, crosses the Tygart River. Built in 1852 by Lemuel and Eli Chenoweth, it is West Virginia's oldest and longest covered bridge still in use. Not far away was the site of the first land battle of the Civil War.

2. Mud River Covered Bridge

    This 108-foot-5-inch bridge over the Mud River is located at the junction of Route 60 and Secondary Route 25 in Milton. Built in 1876 by R. H. Baker, the bridge is in fair condition. West Virginia historian John Alexander Williams has recommended this bridge and the next one as worth a visit.

3. Indian Creek Covered Bridge

    Near Salt Sulphur Springs on Route 219 across from St. John's Church, this bridge was built in 1903 by Ray and Oscar Weikel and E. P. and A. P. Smith. It is 49 feet, 3 inches long and is open to pedestrians only. The original construction cost was $400.

All seventeen of West Virginia's covered bridges are worth a visit. This one is the Dents Run Covered Bridge, near Morgantown.

4. Laurel Creek Covered Bridge
    Winding back roads off Route 219 (specifically, 219/7 and (219/11) lead to Lillydale. Beyond Lillydale, spanning Locust Creek, is West Virginia's shortest covered bridge, 24 feet, 5 inches, built by Robert Annott in 1911. Still in use, it is in only fair condition.

5. Locust Creek Covered Bridge
    This handsome bridge, which has been featured in West Virginia promotional literature, crosses Locust Creek about 6.3 miles south of Hillsboro on Secondary Route 31. An unknown builder in the 1870s did an excellent job, for this 113-foot-9-inch bridge is still in use and is in good shape.

10 West Virginia Lakes Created by Federal Dams

The federal government constructed a number of dams in the Ohio River Valley to provide both flood control and recreation. These ten lakes were formed.

1. Beech Fork Lake
2. Bluestone Lake
3. Burnsville Lake
4. East Lynn Lake
5. Jennings Randolph Lake
6. R. D. Bailey Lake
7. Stonewall Jackson Lake
8. Summersville Lake
9. Sutton Lake
10. Tygart Lake

4 Endangered Plant Species in West Virginia

1. Shale barren rockcress
    A member of the mustard family, tall, slender and herbaceous, shale barren rockcress has been ranked by the Natural Heritage System as "critically imperilled globally." It exists at only 18 known sites in West Virginia and 13 in Virginia. The plant blossoms in April and May, producing tiny white flowers.

2. Running buffalo clover
    This species of the legume family was once common from West Virginia to eastern Kansas, but until recently was thought to be extinct. In 1983 and 1984 two small populations were found, one beside an off-road vehicle trail in the New River Gorge [Fayette], the other at the edge of a field near the Back Fork, Elk River [Webster].

3. Harperella
    Harperella is a delicate annual of the carrot family that grows in a number of Southeastern states. Critically imperilled in West Virginia, the two known sites are along Sleepy Creek and Cacapon River in Morgan County. The umbels of this species resemble those of Queen Anne's lace.

4. Virginia spiraea
    This is a shrub in the rose family that has been found in six Southeastern states. Of the eleven sites in West Virginia, the Gauley River populations may be the world's most extensive. Other sites are along the Bluestone, Meadow, Greenbrier, and Buckhannon Rivers.

8 Endangered Wildlife Species in West Virginia

West Virginia has no state legislation concerning endangered species. The animals below are designated "Endangered" by the U.S. Fish and Wildlife Service under the provisions of the Endangered Species Act of 1973.

1. Peregrine falcon

    The peregrine falcon, once common in West Virginia, declined rapidly in the 1940s and 1950s primarily because of the use of DDT. Captive breeding has led to the limited reintroduction of the peregrine falcon into the Mountain State.

2. Bald eagle

    Not until 1981 was the first recorded nest for this bird, our national symbol, found in West Virginia, in Hardy County. Bald eagles, like peregrine falcons, were decimated by DDT but are making a gradual comeback. There are now three recorded nests in the state.

3. Virginia big-eared bat

    Found in small, scattered groups in West Virginia, Virginia, Kentucky, and North Carolina, this subspecies of Townsend's big-eared bat needs caves to rear their young in the summer and to hibernate in the winter. The state has some 7,350 big-eared bats.

4. Indiana bat

    A Midwestern resident with a population of about 5,950 in West Virginia, this bat usually rears its young under the loose bark of trees. In the winter it hibernates in caves, where it must not be disturbed. Most caves that harbor these bats have been gated or fenced.

5. Gray bat
    The endangered gray bat was first spotted in the Mountain State in the winter of 1990-91.

6. Eastern cougar
    This species, once found throughout the Eastern United States, was nearly wiped out by the late 1880s. West Virginia's Wildlife Resources Section (WRS) receives dozens of cougar reports annually from throughout the state. Yet there is no absolute proof of their present existence in the state.

7. Northern flying squirrel
    Many flying squirrels live in the state, but nearly all of them are southern flying squirrels. The northern species, extremely rare, is listed as endangered in West Virginia, Virginia, North Carolina, and Tennessee. Northern flying squirrels are slightly larger than their southern cousins and have white-tipped gray belly hairs.

8. Freshwater mussels
    Actually, these should be counted as five endangered species—(1) pink mucket pearly mussel, (2) tuberculed-blossom pearly mussel, (3) ringpink, (4) James spinymussel, and (5) fanshell. All but the James spinymussel are found in large rivers such as the Ohio and Kanawha. The James spinymussel occurs in small headwater tributaries of the James River.

8 Historic West Virginia Houses

1. General Adam Stephen House (Martinsburg)
    Completed in 1789, more than seven decades before West Virginia became a state, this two-story house of native limestone, still with its original wooden floors, was home to Scottish-born surgeon Adam Stephen, a veteran of the Revolution and the founder of Martinsburg.

2. Alexander Campbell Mansion (Bethany)
    Campbell, an important 19th-century religious leader and founder of Bethany College, lived in this 22-room house but wrote his sermons in a small, separate, hexagonal study nearby on the grounds. The mansion, owned by the college, is just up the road from "God's Acre," the Campbell family cemetery.

3. Blennerhassett Mansion (near Parkersburg)
    This magnificent Italian Palladium style mansion was originally built in the late 1790s. It burned in 1811 and was reconstructed in the 1980s on its original site on Blennerhassett Island. The ill-fated Blennerhassetts, Harman and Margaret, were caught up in the Aaron Burr conspiracy in 1805.

4. Craik-Patton House (Charleston)
    First known as Elm Grove, this attractive house was built in 1834 by James Craik, a lawyer turned Episcopal priest. It was bought by George Smith Patton, a lawyer and forebear of the great World War II general. Twice moved, the house was carefully restored in the 1970s.

5. Henderson Hall (near Williamstown)

    A three-story Italianate villa style mansion, Henderson Hall was first built in 1836, then added to 20 years later. Through generations, the family members saved everything, so that today their impressive home is a treasure trove of historic relics and memorabilia.

6. Berkeley Castle (Berkeley Springs)

    In 1885 Colonel Samuel Taylor Suit had this replica of Berkeley Castle in England built of hand-carved sandstone for his young bride. She entertained lavishly, her husband's fortunes dwindled, and the place fell into disrepair. In 1954 Walter Bird bought it and restored it.

7. Halliehurst (Elkins)

    Charles T. Mott, a New York architect, designed this three-story model of a castle on the Rhine for Stephen Benton Elkins, a coal and timber baron who married Hallie, the daughter of Senator Henry G. Davis. The grand residence, completed before the turn of the century, belongs to Davis and Elkins College.

8. Governor's Mansion (Charleston)

    The 30-room Governor's Mansion in Charleston, part of the Capitol Complex, is a handsome, Georgian-style building funded by the taxpayers of West Virginia. It was designed by William F. Martens, a Charleston architect. Construction began in 1924, and Governor Ephraim F. Morgan moved in a year later.

—Source: *The West Virginia One-Day Trip Book*
by Suzanne Lord and Jon Metzger

7 West Virginia Churches Worth a Special Visit

Every church is worth a special visit, of course, but the seven on this list have features or associations that set them apart.

1. Old Bethany Meeting House (Bethany)
    Sited on land donated by Alexander Campbell, founder of Bethany College and the Disciples of Christ, this 1850 brick church was in use until 1915. From its pulpit, Campbell preached to a congregation separated by sex. Guided tours require an appointment.

2. First Presbyterian Church (Charleston)
    The architectural firm of Wever-Werner-Atkins designed this 1915 landmark West Virginia church. Located at the corner of Broad and Virginia Streets, it features an imperial Roman exterior and a magnificent Byzantine interior, including a handsome dome 52 feet in diameter.

3. African Zion Baptist Church (Malden)
    This is the mother church of African American Baptists in West Virginia. Built in 1872, it was the church that Booker T. Washington attended between the ages of nine and sixteen.

4. Old Stone Church (Lewisburg)
    A Presbyterian church built in 1796—and thus the oldest church building west of the Alleghenies in continuous use—this historic structure was originally 40 x 40 feet. Later enlarged, the building has a severe gray limestone exterior, but its interior is warm and welcoming.

5. Old Rehoboth Church (near Union)
> One of the ten designated Methodist shrines in the United States, this log church on Route 3 two miles east of Union was dedicated in 1786. It once served as a fort on the Indian frontier. The church has a small museum, with no admission charge.

6. Andrews Methodist Episcopal Church (Grafton)
> This two-story brick church, built in 1873, is designated as the International Mother's Day Shrine. The first Mother's Day service, honoring member Anna Jarvis's mother, in particular, and all mothers generally, was held here on May 10, 1908.

7. Zion Episcopal Church (Charles Town)
> This church, located on Congress Street between Mildred and Church Streets, is a replica of one built earlier. The building housed Union troops during the Civil War. In the graveyard (a National Historic Landmark) are buried some 75 members of the Washington family.

Old Rehoboth Church, near Union, is a Methodist shrine.

4 Distinguished Four-Year Colleges And Universities in West Virginia

West Virginia has a number of excellent colleges and universities. These four are among the best in several respects—in academic reputation, honored history, and attractive settings.

1. Bethany College (Bethany)
    Founded in 1840 by Alexander Campbell, a minister whose preachings gave rise to the Disciples of Christ, Bethany is a private liberal arts college with about 750 students. Its 300-acre campus has many historic buildings. The Old Main building is its centerpiece.

2. Shepherd College (Shepherdstown)
    An attractive public liberal arts college with about 2,300 students, Shepherd was founded in 1871 as a teachers' college. Its location, about 70 miles from Baltimore and Washington, and its low cost have made it a popular and growing institution.

3. West Virginia University (Morgantown)
    Unquestionably the best-known institution of higher learning in the state, WVU, founded in 1867, has about 15,000 full-time undergraduates at Morgantown. Its Personal Rapid Transit System (PRT) is unique. Several small, specialized museums are on campus.

4. West Virginia Wesleyan College (Buckhannon)
    Affiliated with the United Methodist Church, this college of 1,450 students features Gothic architecture on its 80-acre campus. Wesley Chapel, the largest church in the state, has a Casavant organ with 1,474 pipes.

5 Alternate-Use Buildings in West Virginia

An alternate-use building is one built for a particular purpose but later serving another—a one-time railroad station now a restaurant; an old public library now a bookstore. There are so many such buildings in West Virginia that this list merely scratches the surface. You will easily find other examples.

1. Trans Allegheny Books (Parkersburg)
    This impressive bookstore, specializing in rare and used books, occupies what was once Parkersburg's Andrew Carnegie Public Library, built in 1906.

2. Heritage Station (Huntington)
    A railroad station built in 1887, this building at 11th Street and Veterans Memorial Boulevard is now a fine restaurant, listed in the *Mobil Travel Guide*.

3. Pence Springs Hotel (Pence Springs)
    The Pence Springs Hotel opened in 1918 and prospered until the Depression. Closed for 12 years, it reopened in 1947 as a state prison for women and remained one until 1983. In 1989 it opened once more as a hotel.

4. Pocahontas County Tourist Commission (Marlinton)
    The Commission is housed in the old C & O Railroad building, now painted a cheerful yellow, on Route 39.

5. Yellow Brick Bank (Shepherdstown)
    On the corner of German and Princess Streets, this 1910 bank building is now a restaurant, offering lunch and dinner rather than savings and checking accounts.

7 Important West Virginia Museums

1. The Cultural Center (Charleston)
    Part of the Capitol Complex, the Cultural Center is a large, modern building that houses an array of attractions: art and historical exhibits, various research libraries, the Great Hall, the State Theater, the State Museum, and the State Archives Library. The Mountain Stage broadcasts music nationwide on Sundays.

2. Sunrise Museum (Charleston)
    Across the South Side Bridge are two mansions built by William A. MacCorkle, governor from 1893 to 1897. One of the mansions is now an Art Museum, featuring 19th and 20th century works; the other is a Children's Museum, with a nature center, planetarium, and gardens. The estate offers a superb view of Charleston.

3. Huntington Museum of Art (Huntington)
    This impressive art museum offers European and American paintings, Ohio Valley art glass, Appalachian folk art, and the Dean firearms collection. It occupies more than fifty acres of land, with nature trails, herb gardens, a sculpture garden, and an amphitheater.

4. West Virginia State Farm Museum (Point Pleasant)
    Started in 1976, this museum consists of more than thirty period buildings, depicting early rural life in West Virginia. Among them are a log house, a one-room schoolhouse, an old-time post office, and a country store. A mounted horse, General, is reputedly the third largest horse that ever lived.

5. Youth Museum of Southern West Virginia (Beckley)
    This modest museum on the grounds of New River Park presents hands-on exhibits in a space constructed from four railroad boxcars. In addition to a planetarium, a John Henry exhibit contains more than 100 folk-art carvings showing railroad work in the 1880s.

6. Pearl S. Buck Birthplace Museum (Hillsboro)
    The Nobel Prize and Pulitzer Prize-winning author of *The Good Earth* was born here in 1892. The house has been restored to its appearance at that time. The interior is furnished with period pieces, some of them handcrafted by the author's grandfather.

7. Harpers Ferry National Historical Park (Harpers Ferry)
    Occupying more than 2,200 acres, this park, in its picturesque setting, is the state's most visited attraction. The town, largely restored, was the scene of John Brown's raid in 1859 and was a strategic objective in the Civil War. Scenery, museums, restored houses, and historic sights are among the many things to see.

Businesses

Weirton Steel is the largest private employer in West Virginia—and the world's biggest employee-owned steel company.

10 Largest Private Employers in West Virginia

1. Weirton Steel Corporation
2. The Kroger Co.
3. Charleston Area Medical Center
4. E. I. Du Pont De Nemours & Company
5. Chesapeake and Potomac
6. Union Carbide
7. Consolidation Coal Company
8. Appalachian Power Company
9. Eastern Associated Coal Corp.
10. Kmart Corporation

9 Famous Brand-Name Products Manufactured in West Virginia

These are just a few of the products with household names that are made in the state. Glassware has a separate list.

1. Ames garden tools (Parkersburg)
2. Corningware (Martinsburg)
3. Eagle fuel cans (Wellsburg)
4. Hanover shoes (Franklin)
5. Kingsford charcoal briquets (Parsons)
6. Laughlin china (Newell)
7. Mail Pouch tobacco (Wheeling)
8. Sterling faucets (Morgantown)
9. Wheeling steel pails (Wheeling)

11 Railroads in West Virginia

Class I roads

1. CSX. Formerly the merged C&O and B&O (at first called the Chessie System)
2. Norfolk Southern. Formerly the Norfolk & Western and the Virginian.
3. Conrail. Formerly the New York Central.

Short lines—interstate

4. Wheeling & Lake Erie
5. Winchester & Western

Short lines—intrastate

6. Beech Mountain (8 miles)
7. Buffalo Creek & Gauley (19 miles)
8. Elk Valley (67 miles)
9. Little Kanawha River Rail (3 miles)
10. South Branch Valley Rail (56 miles)
11. Winifrede (7 miles)

The Great Trunk Lines

In the glory days of American railroading, from the Civil War through World War II, the major trunk lines in West Virginia were the Baltimore & Ohio (B&O), Chesapeake and Ohio (C&O), and Norfolk and Western (N&W).

4 Once-Prosperous Industries in West Virginia

1. Salt (Malden)

    Salt springs, well known to American Indians in the Kanawha Valley, had become big business by 1815. Thirty salt furnaces dotted the valley. More than 3,000 people worked in the Kanawha salt industry. A saltmakers trust, established to protect the owners, failed to do so, and outside competition did in most operators by the end of the Civil War.

2. Wooden clothespins, heels for women's shoes (Richwood, Rainelle)

    Not surprisingly, West Virginia had a thriving logging industry and bustling lumber towns. The industry still exists, but many of the products are no longer viable. Richwood once led the world in clothespin production. Rainelle turned out more than 4,000,000 women's wooden shoe heels annually. No more.

3. Wooden and steel-hulled boats (Point Pleasant)

    As writers for the WPA noted during the Depression, Point Pleasant for "more than 150 years . . . has depended on the moods of the rivers for bread and butter, for conversation, for periodic excitement." It also depended on the boat-building industry for jobs, but that source of prosperity has now fled.

4. Airplanes (Glen Dale)

    Starting in 1928, Fokker Trimotors in Glendale built 59 model F-10As—the kind of airplane in which Knute Rockne was killed in a 1931 crash in Kansas. Prior to the advent of DC-2s and DC-3s, these F10As were the leading planes for U.S. airlines. The last one built, the "Josephine Ford" (named for Henry Ford's daughter), hangs in the Ford Museum in Dearborn, Michigan.

9 Companies with Large Land Holdings In West Virginia

This list, two decades old, appeared in the "Bicentennial Salute" issue of *The West Virginia Hillbilly*. It serves to emphasize the absentee-landlord status of much of the nonpublic land in West Virginia. (Company headquarters are in parentheses.)

1. Consolidation Coal Company. (Continental Oil Co., Pittsburgh, PA) 554,097 acres in 10 counties
2. Chessie System, Inc. (now CSX, Stamford, CT) 517,636 acres in 18 counties
3. Norfolk and Western Railway Co. (now Norfolk Southern, Norfolk, VA) 443,331 in 6 counties)
4. Georgia Pacific Corp. (Portland, OR) 377,308 acres in 10 counties)
5. Columbia Gas System (Wilmington, DE) 326,306 acres in 4 counties)
6. Westvaco Corp. (New York, NY) 272,262 acres in 14 counties
7. Eastern Gas and Fuel Associates (Boston, MA) 263,025 acres in 13 counties.
8. Cabot, Inc. (Boston, MA) 136,995 acres in 13 counties
9. Bethlehem Steel Corp. (Bethlehem, PA) 128,050 acres in 10 counties

12 Totals by Decade Showing Changes in West Virginia's Coal Industry

This list provides a concise outline of the changes in the coal and coke industry in West Virginia from 1880 through 1990.

	Year	Employees	Coal tons	Fatalities
1.	1880	3,726	1,829,844	--
2.	1890	11,497	7,394,564	39
3.	1900	29,017	22,647,207	141
4.	1910	68,135	59,274,708	320
5.	1920	97,426	89,590,271	320
6.	1930	107,832	122,429,767	412
7.	1940	130,457	126,619,825	376
8.	1950	119,568	145,563,295	185
9.	1960	48,696	120,107,994	115
10.	1970	45,261	143,132,284	63
11.	1980	55,502	121,583,762	33
12.	1990	28,876	171,155,053	12

Population Loss in the Coal Counties

As employees in the mines lost their jobs, people moved away from the coal regions. In some counties the population loss was devastating. The number of people in McDowell County declined from 98,887 in 1950 to 35,323 in 1990. In Fayette County the population dropped from 82,443 to 47,952.

9 Notable West Virginia Glass Factories

There were once more than a hundred glassmaking operations in West Virginia, but the number has been drastically reduced over the years. The nine that follow are not the only glassmaking enterprises left in the state, but they are among the most impressive. They offer tours (sometimes by appointment), gift shops, and, at Blenko and Fenton, glass museums.

1. Blenko Glass Company (Milton)
   Founded in 1922 by a British glassmaker, this factory is internationally famous for its handblown glassware and blown stained glass, with installations worldwide.

2. Brooke Glass Company (Wellsburg)
   This small, hand-operated factory produces a variety of glass products, including lamps and candle holders. It also does custom matching of antique pieces.

3. Dalzell-Viking (New Martinsville)
   Famous for handmade colored glassware, Dalzell-Viking, established in 1884, is one of the state's oldest glass manufacturers.

4. Fenton Art Glass Factory and Museum (Williamstown)
   Employing approximately 350 full-time workers, Fenton has been turning out colorful and elegant glassware since 1907. The factory tour is outstanding.

5. Gentile Glass Company (Star City)
   Although the small staff at Gentile specializes in glass paperweights, they also produce custom monogrammed crystal glassware and other items.

6. The Glass Swan (Jane Lew)
    In addition to producing cobalt blue tableware, The Glass Swan specializes in making glass marbles in a dazzling variety of designs.

7. Hamon Glass Studio (Scott Depot)
    The husband-and-wife team who own this studio specialize in paperweights, glass sculpture, and blown art glass.

8. Mid-Atlantic Glass Factory (Ellenboro)
    Glass marbles and small handmade and blown glass items like wine glasses and vases are made at this little factory just a few minutes off Route 50.

9. Pilgrim Glass Corporation (Ceredo)
    This famous glassmaking concern attracts thousands of visitors a year. Two of its best-known specialties are the popular, costly Cranberry Glass and Cameo Glass.

4 Old Country Stores in West Virginia

1. Harper's Old Country Store (Seneca Rocks)
    Located at the junction of Routes 33 and 28 in Pendleton County, this store has been run by the Harper family since 1902. If you need it, it's here—clothing, beer, gasoline, bait, souvenirs, hunting and fishing licenses, or pizza from an attached restaurant.

2. Berdine's Variety Store (Harrisville)
    Berdine's moved to its present location at 106 Court Street in 1915 after its founding nearby in 1908. It is West Virginia's, and possibly the nation's, oldest five-and-dime. The variety of low-priced merchandise is endless—candy, pots and pans, cow bells, oil lamps.

3. Sharp's Country Store (Slatyfork)
    On Rt. 219, four miles south of Snowshoe Ski Resort, Sharp's has been doing business here since 1927. A well-stocked general store with an impressive memorabilia collection, it offers maple syrup, fresh bait, gasoline, T-shirts, hand-dipped ice cream . . . you name it.

4. O'Hurley's General Store (Shepherdstown)
    Fifty years ago, Jay Hurley's father ran a gas station here. Today the building at 205 E. Washington St. (on Rt. 230) is a neatly recreated turn-of-the century general store with a prodigious array of wares, some locally produced, some from suppliers worldwide.

10 West Virginia Bed & Breakfasts

Once upon a time, a tourist home—a private house with one or more rooms for overnight guests—was an inexpensive alternative to a hotel. No valet parking, no bellhop—no frills. Then motels came on the scene, followed by motor hotels. A few tourist homes managed to struggle on in isolated areas. But, by and large, the tourist-home business was gone—until some bright entrepreneur hit upon the idea of "bed and breakfast." Voila! "B&B" was the old tourist home reborn, now with a home-cooked meal. Very *au courant.* Today the B&B flourishes, typically as a pleasant, sometimes upscale alternative to hotels, motels, and other impersonal accommodations. The ten B&Bs on this list each have at least five rooms for guests. All serve a full breakfast.

1. Highlawn Inn (Berkeley Springs)
    A Victorian house at 304 Market Street, the Highlawn Inn has six guest rooms, offers a full country breakfast, and will serve dinner by reservation. (304) 258-5700.

2. Cottonwood Inn (Charles Town)
    Near Harpers Ferry at Mill Lane and Cable Town Road, this country inn has seven guest rooms, a sitting room, and a library. (304) 725-3371.

3. Hillbrook Inn (Charles Town)
    On Route 13 at Summit Point Road, this European-style country inn, with five guest rooms, is a jewel in a lovely woodland setting. (304) 725-4223.

4. Bright Morning (Davis)
    A former boarding house on William Avenue, Davis's

main street, the restored building accommodates 18 guests in seven bedrooms, one suite. (304) 259-5119.

5. Retreat at Buffalo Run (Elkins)
At 214 Harpertown Road, this gracious turn-of-the-century home, with seven guest rooms, is surrounded by trees and rhododendrons. (304) 636-2960.

6. Dunn Country Inn (Martinsburg)
An 1805 home on the National Register, the Dunn Country Inn, located in a serene setting on Route 3, has five guest rooms. (304) 263-8646.

7. Hampshire House 1884 (Romney)
Completely renovated, with a sitting room, library and period furniture, this 1884 home offers gourmet dining with a fine wine list. (304) 822-7171.

8. Thomas Shepherd Inn (Shepherdstown)
An 1868 home in an historic Civil War town, the Thomas Shepherd Inn has six guest rooms and a living room with fireplace. (304) 876-3715.

9. The Elk River Inn (Slatyfork)
A farmhouse and an inn, each with five guest rooms, plus a private cabin with two bedrooms make up this B&B complex. (304) 572-3771.

10. Yesterdays, Ltd. (Wheeling)
Restored Victorian townhouses in an historic district overlooking the river just off I-70 offer 26 guest rooms furnished with antiques. (304) 232-0864.

7 Three-Star Restaurants in West Virginia

These rankings are from the *Mobil Travel Guide: Middle Atlantic States.* A three-star ranking means "excellent." There is also a four-star restaurant in West Virginia, outranking all those on this list—"outstanding" and "worth a special visit," according to the Mobil rating system. It is the Main Dining Room of The Greenbrier resort in White Sulphur Springs.

1. Ernie's Esquire (Wheeling)
    On Bethlehem Boulevard, 1¼ miles off I-70 on Route 88-S, Ernie's Esquire features a continental menu. Each of the six rooms has a different decor. (304) 242-2800.

2. Rebels & Redcoats Tavern (Huntington)
    At 626 West 5th Street, this restaurant, with colonial decor and a fireplace, offers specialities that include veal Oscar and châteaubriand bouquetière. (304) 523-8829.

3. Chilton House (St. Albans)
    Occupying a restored 1847 Gothic revival house with antiques and original paintings, the Chilton House is on Sixth Avenue. Its menu is continental. (304) 722-2918.

4. Riverside Inn (Pence Springs)
    On Route 3 east of Hinton, the Riverside Inn, an early 1900s log lodge, has an imaginative menu that includes colonial meat pies and bread pudding. (304) 445-7469.

5. Tiffany's Continental Key Club (Fairmont)
    Tiffany's, on North Bellview Boulevard, offers an Italian and continental menu, with specialties of beef Wellington and veal parmigiana. (304) 363-7859.

6. Jim Reid's (Nutter Fort)
    At 1422 Buckhannon Pike, just south of Clarksburg, Jim Reid's specializes in fresh seafood, steak, and prime rib. (304) 623-4909.

7. Bavarian Inn and Lodge (Shepherdstown)
    In an elegant inn overlooking the Potomac River, this restaurant features a varied German continental menu, with sauerbraten and game in season. It also serves vegetarian dishes and fresh seafood. (304) 876-2551.

10 West Virginia Wineries

West Virginia wines can be found in many local grocery stores and restaurants. Some wineries exhibit at West Virginia fairs and festivals. Visitors are generally welcome, but it is advisable to call ahead, because not all are open the whole year.

1. A. T. Gift Winery (Harpers Ferry) (304) 876-6680.
2. Fisher Ridge Wines (Liberty) (304) 342-8702.
3. Forks of Cheat Winery (Morgantown) (304) 598-2019.
4. Kirkwood Limited (Summersville) (304) 872-2134.
5. Laurel Creek Winery (Lewisburg) (304) 645-6552.
6. Robert F. Pliska Winery (Purgitsville) (304) 289-3493.
7. Potomac Highland Winery (Keyser) (304) 788-3066.
8. Schneider's Winery (Romney) (304) 822-7434.
9. Tentchurch Vineyard (Colliers) (304) 527-3916.
10. West-Whitehill Winery (Moorefield) (304) 538-2605.

3 Places to Dine in West Virginia That Have Items Setting Them Apart

These are author Dick Weigen's choices after traveling the highways and byways of West Virginia for many years.

1. General Lewis Inn (Lewisburg)
    The dining room at the General Lewis Inn, 301 East Washington Street (U.S. Route 60), offers a unique and superb poppy-seed salad dressing.

2. Elk River Inn (Gassaway)
    At the Elk River Inn's dining room, Route 4, diners are treated to a barbeque sauce unlike any other, fresh or bottled. Not for the faint of heart, it's got a bite.

3. Oliverio's (Bridgeport)
    On U.S. Route 50 in Bridgeport, Oliverio's provides a never-ending supply of breadsticks. If one *could* live on bread alone, this would be the bread.

3 Early West Virginia Spas Still in Business

1. Berkeley Springs

    George Washington took the waters here to gain relief from rheumatic fever. The springs, which discharge 2,000 gallons of water a minute at a constant temperature of 74.3° F., were believed by the Indians to have therapeutic powers. Berkeley Springs State Park encompasses the springs and offers health baths of various kinds. Nominal fees are charged for the use of the baths and for various forms of physiotherapy, such as infrared heat, steam cabinets, and massage.

2. The Greenbrier (White Sulphur Springs)

    Dating from the early 1800s (although its "curative" waters" were known well before that), this five-star resort with its "magic fountain" has attracted the wealthy and famous for nearly 200 years. More than half the Presidents of the United States have vacationed here. A separate list (page 137) shows some of the history of The Greenbrier.

3. Pence Springs

    Since 1872 there have been three hotels at the site, the latest once built in 1918, just after World War I. The spa boomed during the 'twenties, with as many as 14 trains arriving daily during the summer. Then, in 1935, the Depression killed it, and in 1947 the hotel reopened as a women's prison. That venture ended in 1985 for lack of certain facilities. Remarkably, a private investor purchased the property, restored the hotel, and opened it once again for business.

5 West Virginia Resorts of Yesteryear

A fashionable "tour of the waters" in the 1800s would also have included White Sulphur Springs, Green Sulphur Springs, Gray Sulphur Springs, Blue Sulphur Springs, Warm Springs, and Hot Springs.

1. Red Sulphur Springs

    One of the great (but less expensive) health and social resorts of its time, Red Sulphur Springs boasted a large hotel that opened in 1832. During the Civil War, the building served as a Confederate hospital. Attempts to revive the resort after the war met with limited success. Levi P. Morton, Vice President under Benjamin Harrison, owned it for a time.

2. Salt Sulphur Springs

    This resort was opened in 1823 and was expanded in 1830. It featured 98 guest rooms, a large ballroom, a dining room, and three springs—the Salt Sulphur, the Sweet, and the Iodine. Presidents Monroe and Van Buren and Senators Calhoun and Clay vacationed here. Confederate generals made it their headquarters during the Civil War. It prospered on and off until 1936.

3. Sweet Springs

    This once-fashionable spa opened in 1792. Renowned as Old Sweet, the resort reached its height after 1833 with the building of a handsome Georgian Colonial hotel based on a design by Thomas Jefferson. Today the old hotel is the Andrew S. Rowan Memorial Home for the Aged.

4. Lee's White Sulphur Springs (near Lost City)

   In the early nineteenth century, Henry (Light Horse Harry) Lee established a hotel on the property. Once a popular resort—particularly after 1879 when it passed out of the Lee family and was rebuilt and expanded—the grounds are now part of the Lost River State Park. (Note that this site in Hardy County is far from the Greenbrier County town of White Sulphur Springs.)

5. Capon Springs

   Discovered by Henry Frye, who moved his family here is 1765, where his wife's rheumatism was cured by the mineral waters. A four-story hotel, the Mountain House, was built in 1849, and the resort prospered. In 1859 Colonel Robert E. Lee was called away from Capon Springs to put down John Brown's raid at Harpers Ferry. Today the springs are privately owned.

Berkeley Springs has been a health resort since colonial times. George Washington bathed in the waters just as visitors do today.

5 Three-Star Resorts in West Virginia

The rankings are from the *Mobil Travel Guide: Middle Atlantic States*. A three-start ranking means "excellent." (The Greenbrier, in a class by itself, has five stars.)

1. Oglebay's Wilson Lodge (Wheeling)
    Wheeling's Oglebay Resort Park is a municipal park on a grand scale—a resort, zoo, museum, arboretum, three 18-hole golf courses, and much more. Nestled in the 1,500-acre park is the 204-room lodge.

2. Sheraton Lakeview Resort and Conference Center (near Morgantown)
    With four swimming pools (two indoors), two 18-hole golf courses, indoor/outdoor tennis, and an exercise room, the Sheraton Lakeview caters to active guests.

3. Pipestem (near Hinton)
    Crown jewel of the state park system, Pipestem is described on page 72.

4. Canaan Valley (near Davis)
    The 6,700-acre Canaan Valley Resort Park is set amidst spectacular mountain scenery. Run on a concession basis by a private firm, it is perhaps best known as a resort ski facility, but summer activities abound, too.

5. The Woods Resort & Conference Center (Hedgesville)
    Twelve miles from Martinsburg, The Woods, somewhat smaller than the resorts above, has a 60-room lodge plus cabins, three swimming pools (one indoors), lighted tennis courts, and 27-hole golf privileges.

7 Noteworthy Facts About The Greenbrier

Although The Greenbrier has vied for leadership through the years with other fine West Virginia spas, it is today the premier resort in West Virginia and is among the finest in the United States. (Before 1913 the resort was called White Sulphur Springs, and the hotel, now gone, became popularly known as "Old White.")

1. The Greenbrier is one of ten resorts that the *Mobil Guide* awards five stars—and the only one in the Middle Atlantic (or Northeast) states.

2. On the exclusive list of Historic Hotels of America, designated by the National Trust for Historic Preservation, The Greenbrier is one of two in West Virginia. The other is the Blennerhassett Hotel in Parkersburg.

3. Countless celebrities, including 22 Presidents of the United States, have stayed at the resort. Senator Henry Clay of Kentucky was the unofficial host for more than three decades. General Robert E. Lee enjoyed three post-Civil War summers here.

4. President John Tyler, 54, spent part of his honeymoon in 1844 at White Sulphur Springs with his bride, Julia Gardner, 24. President Woodrow Wilson also honeymooned at The Greenbrier, in 1915, with the second Mrs. Wilson.

5. Writers of fiction have used the resort as their setting. Charles Dudley Warner's novel, *Their Pilgrimage*, portrays White Sulphur Springs in its post Civil War

glory. Rex Stout's *Too Many Cooks* (1938), one of the best Nero Wolfe mysteries, features The Greenbrier's chef and his cuisine.

6. In World War II The Greenbrier did its bit, first as an internment center for German and Japanese diplomats before they returned to their countries, and next as Ashford General Hospital, a 2,200-bed military facility. The resort reopened in April 1948.

7. Golf, which was first played in America on a course in White Sulphur Springs (though not at the resort), is a mainstay at The Greenbrier. There are three 18-hole golf courses, including The Greenbrier Course, designed under the direction of Jack Nicklaus. For many years Sam Snead was The Greenbrier's pro.

Arts and Media

Denise Giardina's moving novel, *Storming Heaven*, is one of many fine fictional works set in West Virginia. Giardina is from Bluefield.

23 Daily Newspapers in West Virginia

The circulation figures shown are approximate.

1.	Charleston	*The Charleston Gazette*	54,000
2.	Charleston	*Charleston Daily Mail*	49,000
3.	Huntington	*Herald-Dispatch*	42,000
4.	Beckley	*The Register-Herald*	32,000
5.	Bluefield	*Bluefield Daily Telegraph*	24,000
6.	Wheeling	*The Intelligencer*	23,500
7.	Wheeling	*Wheeling News-Register*	23,000
8.	Parkersburg	*The Parkersburg News*	22,000
9.	Morgantown	*Dominion Post*	21,000
10.	Martinsburg	*The Morning Journal*	18,000
11.	Clarksburg	*Clarksburg Telegram*	15,000
12.	Fairmont	*Times-West Virginian*	14,000
13.	Parkersburg	*The Parkersburg Sentinel*	12,500
14.	Elkins	*The Inter-Mountain*	11,500
15.	Williamson	*Williamson Daily News*	11,000
16.	Logan	*The Logan Banner*	10,000
17.	Weirton	*Weirton Daily Times*	8,500
18.	Welch	*The Welch Daily News*	7,200
19.	Clarksburg	*The Clarksburg Exponent*	6,500
20.	Keyser	*Mineral Daily News Tribune*	6,300
21.	Point Pleasant	*Point Pleasant Register*	5,300
22.	Moundsville	*Moundsville Daily Echo*	4,500
23.	Lewisburg-Ronceverte-White Sulphur Springs	*West Virginia Daily News*	3,900

4 Cities in West Virginia With Two Daily Newspapers

Many mid-sized cities in the United States no longer have both a morning and an evening newspaper. But four cities in West Virginia do—even though the circulation of one of them (*The Clarksburg Exponent*) is a scant 6,500.

1. Charleston
    The Charleston Gazette (morning)
    Charleston Daily Mail (evening)
2. Wheeling
    The Intelligencer (morning)
    Wheeling News-Register (evening)
3. Parkersburg
    The Parkersburg News (morning)
    The Parkersburg Sentinal (evening)
4. Clarksburg
    The Clarksburg Exponent (morning)
    Clarksburg Telegram (evening)

3 Official State Songs

Officially, these three songs rank equally.

1. "The West Virginia Hills"
2. "This Is My West Virginia"
3. "West Virginia, My Home Sweet Home"

A song that qualifies as an unofficial favorite is "Take Me Home, Country Roads," popularized by John Denver.

4 Movies Filmed in West Virginia

Among the recent motion pictures shot wholly or in part in West Virginia are these four.

1. *Pudd'n'head Wilson*, 1984 (Harpers Ferry)
    Starring Ken Howard and Lise Hilboldt, this PBS *American Playhouse* film is a excellent adaptation of Mark Twain's tragicomic novel. Leonard Maltin's *TV Movies and Video Guide* rates the production Above Average.

2. *Reckless*, 1984 (Weirton)
    Aidan Quinn and Daryl Hannah star in this film about alienated youth. Jack Barth in his sometimes acerbic book, *Roadside Hollywood,* writes, "The rusty red clouds that hover above this fragrant burg set the hopeless tone for our heroes."

3. *Sweet Dreams*, 1985 (Martinsburg)
    This bio of country singer Patsy Cline features Jessica Lange lip-syncing Cline's recordings. The singer's unhappy marriage to a nogoodnik, played by Ed Harris, dominates the film. Cline's actual hometown was Winchester, Virginia.

4. *Matewan*, 1987 (Thurmond)
    An outstanding film directed by John Sayles, *Matewan* is set not in Matewan but in Thurmond. No matter. Chris Cooper, Will Oldham, Mary McDonnell, Bob Gunton, James Earl Jones, and others perform brilliantly in this story of labor unrest in the coalfields. The photography is eye-catching.

5 Novels with West Virginia Settings

Since a great many novels have been set in West Virginia, this is hardly a comprehensive list. It is an impressive list, however, for these novels all drew rave reviews.

1. *The Night of the Hunter*, by Davis Grubb, 1953

    Davis Grubb's first and most famous novel concerns the testing of a nine-year-old boy, John, entrusted with a dangerous secret. The *Chicago Tribune* reviewer praised Grubb's evocation of "the magic of the changing seasons in the Ohio Valley" and lauded "the deft manner in which the author has succeeded in projecting a dramatic tale of life through the elemental simplicity of childhood."

2. *The Knife in My Hands*, Keith Maillard, 1982

    A reviewer for *American Scene* praised this novel, Maillard's third, as "an eloquent examination of the storms of adolescence. Set in a small town in West Virginia in the late 1950s, [it] chronicles the coming of age of John Dupre, a fiercely intelligent, nonconformist disciple of James Dean searching for his sexual identity."

3. *Machine Dreams*, Jayne Anne Phillips, 1984

    Renowned authors Nadine Gordimer and Anne Tyler praised *Machine Dreams* extravagantly. The novel is the story of the Hampsons, a family from "Bellington," West Virginia, that is falling apart without quite knowing why. The reviewer for the *Washington Post Book World* described *Machine Dreams* as "an elegiac, wistful, rueful book."

4. *Storming Heaven*, by Denise Giardina, 1987
    In the words of noted author Annie Dillard, "This is the gripping story of a real conflict: coal miners and hired gunhands who fought the Battle of Blair Mountain in 1921. Denise Giardina tells the miners' stirring story with fierceness and passion." *Storming Heaven* paints a vivid picture of life in the coal camps and in the town of "Annadel" in "Justice" County, West Virginia.

5. *Dogs of God*, by Pinckney Benedict, 1994.
    High praise greeted short-story-writer Pinckney Benedict's first novel, *Dogs of God*, a fast-paced tale of violence set in rural West Virginia. The *New York Times Book Review* critic called it "stunning," a novel that "tells an amazing story about forces of evil so dark and malevolent that one worries for the sanity of the storyteller who dared look the devils in the eye." It is written "in a vein of rare, wild beauty."

3 Short Story Collections That Feature West Virginia

1. *Uncle Abner, Master of Mysteries*, by Melville Davisson Post. New York: D. Appleton, 1918.
    Uncle Abner, a God-fearing man of absolute integrity, lives in the rugged backwoods of what is now West Virginia at the time of Jefferson's presidency. Abner, a man of brilliant intellect, with a profound knowledge of the Bible, solves cleverly conceived and well-written mysteries. "An Act of God" is one of his best.

2. *Twelve Tales of Suspense and the Supernatural,* by Davis Grubb. New York: Scribner's, 1964.

Not all twelve tales are set in "Cresap's Landing," West Virginia, a town in the Ohio River Valley (presumably somewhere near Moundsville, Grubb's hometown), but several of them are, including the opening short story, "Busby's Rat," and the final one, "Where the Woodbine Twineth."

3. *The Stories of Breece D'J Pancake,* by Breece D'J Pancake. Boston: Atlantic/Little, Brown, 1983.

Pancake, who took his own life at the age of 26, achieved his high reputation posthumously with widespread acclaim for his only collection. His stories show rural West Virginia as a bleak area of rundown farms, abandoned cars, and hard-drinking, resigned men. "Trilobites" is often cited as his finest story.

4 Periodicals About West Virginia

1. *Wonderful West Virginia*

    A beautifully illustrated monthly magazine published by the West Virginia Division of Natural Resources, Capitol Complex, Charleston, WV 25305-0669, the emphasis in on conservation, natural history, outdoor activities, and state history. Circulation: 65,000.

2. *Goldenseal*

    Published by the West Virginia Department of Education and the Arts, Division of Culture and History,

Goldenseal, a quarterly magazine, concentrates on traditional life, folklife, and oral history of West Virginia. Editorial office: 1900 Kanawha Boulevard E., Charleston, WV 25305-0300. Circulation: 33,000.

3. *West Virginia Hillbilly*

    A tabloid-size weekly newspaper, *West Virginia Hillbilly* is aimed at "West Virginians in particular and hill-loving people everywhere." It focuses on American (and specifically West Virginian) history and life. Editorial office: Box 430, Richwood, WV 26261-0430. Circulation: 7,000.

4. *West Virginia History*

    This is a quarterly publication of the West Virginia Department of Education and the Arts, Division of Culture and History (same address as *Goldenseal*). More scholarly than the other magazines listed, its emphasis is indicated by its title.

6 West Virginia Professional Arts Groups

1. Wheeling Symphony (Wheeling)
    The Wheeling Symphony—"the Greatest Little Orchestra in the World"—performs under the musical direction of Rachael Worby. Throughout the year it presents both classical and popular programs at the Capitol Music Hall, 1015 Main Street. Broadway star Mark McVey has appeared as a guest. (304) 232-6100.

2. Huntington Chamber Orchestra (Huntington)
    Conducted by Michael McArtor, this orchestra, established in 1971, performs a classical series of concerts at the JSC Auditorium and the Huntington Museuem of Art during the winter and a Pops Series at Harris Riverfront Park during the summer. Brilliant violinist Sergio Schwartz performed in 1994. (304) 525-0670.

3. Charleston Ballet (Charleston)
    Organized in 1956 by Andre Van Damme, former premier danseur etoile of the Brussels Royal Opera and one of Europe's leading male dancers, the Charleston Ballet is the Official West Virginia State Ballet. Directed by Kim Pauley since 1989, the group performs at the Civic Center Theater. (304) 342-6541.

4. West Virginia Symphony Orchestra (Charleston)
    This 90-piece symphony orchestra, conducted by Thomas Conlin, offers live performances at the Charleston Municipal Auditorium. In 1994-95 it featured such guest artists as violinist Glenn Dicterow, trombonist Christian Lindberg, harpist Melody Rapier, and guitarist Sharon Isbin. (304) 342-0160.

5. Theatre West Virginia (Beckley)
    This professional performing arts theater company presents outdoor musical dramas in Cliffside Amphitheatre, Grandview Park. It also sponsors two touring companies that offer outreach performing arts programs to schools throughout West Virginia and surrounding states. (304) 256-6800.

6. Greenbrier Valley Theatre (Lewisburg)
    For nearly three decades the Greenbrier Valley Theatre has brought together theatre professionals from all over the United States to present musicals, comedies, classic dramas, new works, and plays for children. GVT is a community resource for the arts in the Greenbrier Valley. (304) 645-3838.

6 Active Regional and Community Arts Groups in West Virginia

1. Charleston Light Opera Guild (Charleston)
    Its name notwithstanding, this group produces not operas or operettas, but two Broadway-type musical comedies a year.

2. Kanawha Players (Charleston)
    One one of the oldest community theater groups in the nation, the Kanawha Players—the Official State Theater of West Virginia—dates from 1922. In 1992 it received the Mayor's Award as Arts Organization of the Year.

3. Landmark Studio for the Arts (Sutton)
   Founded in 1988, this group is located in a historic Victorian era church that has been converted into a theater and art space.

4. Lakeview Theatre (Morgantown)
   Lakeview Theatre, whose summer home is the Creative Arts Center on the campus of West Virginia University, features popular musical comedies and original stage productions.

5. Apollo Civic Theatre (Martinsburg)
   Each year this community theater group presents four productions of Broadway's best shows.

6. Old Opera House (Charles Town)
   The Old Opera House Theatre Company, Inc., is a nonprofit community theater that produces seven plays and six guest shows a year.

4 Useful and Appealing Books About West Virginia

There are dozens of fine specialized books that deal, in whole or in part, with West Virginia. Dale Fetherling's *Mother Jones* is excellent, as are Tom Nugent's *Death at Buffalo Creek*, Martin Cherniack's *The Hawk's Nest Incident*, and, on a brighter note, Robert S. Conte's *The History of the Greenbrier*. The books on the next page are more general. They provide a broad and fascinating look at the Mountain State in all its diversity.

1. *West Virginia: A History for Beginners*, by John Alexander Williams. Charleston: Appalachian Editions, 1993.
   Designed as book for teachers and students, this easy-to-read 278-page history presents a clear, comprehensive overview of the state's history. The maps, charts, sidebars, and photos add considerably to its appeal.

2. *West Virginia: A Guide to the Mountain State*, by the Writers' Program of the Work Projects Administration. New York: Oxford University Press, 1941.
   This book is as dated as Williams's is modern, but, like all of the WPA books in the *American Guide Series*, it offers a gold mine of information about the state in the 1930s. All three sections—background, cities, and tours—retain their interest, if not their timeliness.

3. *The West Virginia One-Day Trip Book*, by Suzanne Lord and Jon Metzger. McLean, VA: EPM Publications, 1993.
   One could hardly ask for a better guidebook than this. Well-organized, thoroughly researched, and engagingly written, it covers everything a visitor to the Mountain State, or a peripatetic West Virginian, is likely to want to know.

4. *West Virginia: A History*, by Otis K. Rice. Lexington: University of Kentucky Press, 1984.
   For the reader who wants to delve somewhat deeper than Williams does into the state's history—particularly into the political history—this solid and scholarly account will prove rewarding.

Sports

The Princeton Reds, an Appalachian League affiliate of the Cincinnati Reds, take batting practice at Hunnicutt Field.

6 Baseball Hall-of-Famers Who Played Minor League Baseball in West Virginia

1. Ed Delahanty, 1888 (Wheeling)
   Big Ed Delahanty, one of five brothers who played major league baseball, starred for the Philadelphia Phillies from 1888 to 1901. He began the 1888 season as a second baseman for Wheeling of the Tri-State League. His .408 batting average in 21 games for Wheeling earned him a quick promotion to the majors, where he hit .346 lifetime.

2. Bill McKechnie, 1909 (Wheeling)
   One of the great managers, Bill McKechnie was a weak-hitting third baseman for a number of major and minor league teams—including Wheeling of the Central League—before finding his true calling as a skipper for the Pirates, Cardinals, Braves, and Reds. In his third season of pro ball at Wheeling he batted .274.

3. Lefty Grove, 1920 (Martinsburg)
   The brilliant lefthanded pitcher for the Philadelphia A's and Boston Red Sox tossed his first 59 innings of pro ball for Martinsburg of the Blue Ridge League. His record was 3 wins and 3 losses, hardly what you'd expect of a guy who in 1930-31 would win 59 games and lose only 9 for the A's.

4. Hack Wilson, 1921-22 (Martinsburg)
   Five-and-a-half-foot-tall Hack Wilson holds the major league record for RBIs in a season (190 in 1930) and the National League record for home runs in a season (56 in 1930). An outfielder for the Chicago Cubs, he batted .356 that season as well. At Martinsburg he was a catcher both years, playing in a total of 114 games and batting .365.

5. Walt Alston, 1936 (Huntington)
   First baseman Alston was an outstanding minor leaguer. He cracked a league-leading 35 home runs for Huntington of the Middle Atlantic League in 1936. That was the year he got his only at-bat in the majors. Playing for the St. Louis Cardinals, he struck out. As a manager, he led the Brooklyn and Los Angeles Dodgers in 7 World Series.

6. Stan Musial, 1938-39 (Williamson)
   They thought he was a pitcher, and at first he was, hurling for Williamson of the Mountain State League. He won 6 and lost 6 in 1938 with a 4.66 ERA. Next year he won 9 and lost 2, but his ERA was still a so-so 4.30. The clue to his future as a hard-hitting St. Louis Cardinal outfielder was his batting average in 1939 at Williamson: .352.

6 Places with Fewer Than 4,000 People That Once Had Professional Baseball

Population figures are from the 1990 Census. An x indicates that the team failed to complete the season.

1. Follansbee (3,339) Ohio-Pennsylvania League, 1912x
2. Welch (3,028) Mountain State League, 1937-42; Appalachian League, 1946-55x
3. Montgomery (2,449) Virginia Valley League, 1910; Mountain State League, 1911-12x
4. Logan (2,206) Mountain State League, 1937-42
5. Mannington (2,184) West Virginia League, 1910x
6. Piedmont (1,094) Western Pennsylvania League, 1907x

10 Major League Baseball Players Who Broke in with Bluefield

The following major league team consists entirely of players who have broken into organized baseball since 1959 with the Bluefield Orioles of the Appalachian League.

1. First base: Eddie Murray (batted .287 for Bluefield in 1973). Starred for the Baltimore Orioles, Los Angeles Dodgers, and New York Mets. Eight-time All-Star and probable Hall of Famer.

2. Second base: Bill Ripkin (batted .244 for Bluefield in 1982; .217 in 1983). Younger brother of Cal Ripkin, Jr. Played for the Baltimore Orioles and Texas Rangers.

3. Shortstop: Cal Ripkin, Jr. (batted .264 for Bluefield in 1978). A career Baltimore Oriole, challenging Lou Gehrig for most consecutive games played. American League MVP in 1983 and 1991. Perennial All-Star.

4. Third base: Craig Worthington (batted .341 for Bluefield in 1985). Played for the Baltimore Orioles and Cleveland Indians. AL Rookie of the Year in 1989.

5. Outfield: Boog Powell (batted .351 for Bluefield in 1959). Spent most of his career with the Orioles, finishing up with the Cleveland Indians and L.A. Dodgers. Started as an outfielder but later switched to first base.

6. Outfield: Larry Sheets (batted .267 for Bluefield in 1978; .333 (12 at-bats) in 1979; and .379 in 1980. Spent time with the Orioles but went to Taiyo, Japan, in 1992.

7. Outfield: Don Baylor (batted .346 for Bluefield in 1967). Played mainly for the Orioles and California Angels. Became manager of the new Colorado Rockies in 1993.

8. Catcher: Steve Lake (batted .278 for Bluefield in 1975). Spent many years in the minors before reaching the majors with the Chicago Cubs. Career backup catcher.

9. Right-handed pitcher: Mike Boddicker (2-1, .047 ERA for Bluefield in 1978). Pitched for Baltimore for many years before moving on to Boston and Kansas City. Named AL Rookie Pitcher of the Year in 1983.

10. Left-handed pitcher: Sparky Lyle (3-2, 4.36 ERA for Bluefield in 1964). Premier relief pitcher for various major league teams—Boston Red Sox, New York Yankees, Texas Rangers, and Philadelphia Phillies.

A Manager for Bluefield

If a capable manager is needed, no problem. Bluefield has had several fine skippers. One was Jim Frey, who managed the Rookie Orioles in 1965-66, then went on to lead the Kansas City Royals to an American League pennant in 1980 and the Chicago Cubs to a National League pennant in 1984. Another was Joe Altobelli, who managed Bluefield in 1966-67. He was at the helm of the pennant-winning 1983 Baltimore Orioles.

7 Pro Football Hall of Famers With Ties to West Virginia

These inductees to the Pro Football Hall of Fame in Canton, Ohio, have various kinds of ties to the Mountain State. Gino Marchetti was born in Smithers, Fayette County, but moved away, while Sam Huff played both his high school and college football in the state. Birthplaces are shown in regular type, West Virginia connections in italics.

1. Cliff Battles, 1910-1981 *(Buckhannon)*
    An Ohioan by birth, Battles starred as a halfback at West Virginia Wesleyan College, where he was captain of the football, baseball, basketball, and track teams. He majored in English, and graduated Phi Beta Kappa. His pro football career was with the NFL's Boston Braves and Washington Redskins.

2. Frank Gatski, 1923- (Farmington, *Huntington*)
    "Gunner" Gatski worked for a year in the mines. At Farmington High School he played center, and when Marshall University conducted a tryout in 1940, he tried out. Gatski played for the Cleveland Browns and Detroit Lions.

3. Sam Huff, 1934- (Edna Gas, *Farmington, Morgantown*)
    Robert Lee (Sam) Huff attended Farmington High School and West Virginia University, working his way through college by waiting on tables. A linebacker, he captained the 1955 Mountaineers, made All-America, and was drafted by the New York Giants. He became one of the great linebackers in pro football history.

4. Gino Marchetti, 1927- (Smithers)
   The stellar tackle for the Baltimore Colts might have spent more time in West Virginia, but his family was moved to a California detention camp when Gino was 14. The reason: His father was an Italian immigrant.

5. George Preston Marshall, 1896-1969 (Grafton)
   Marshall made the Pro Football Hall of Fame as an owner, not a player or coach. His team was the NFL's Boston Braves, later the Washington Redskins. Cliff Battles (see above) quit the team at the age of 28 because Marshall refused to give him a $500 raise.

6. Greasy Neale, 1891-1973 (Parkersburg, *Buckhannon, Morgantown*)
   Alfred Earle (Greasy) Neale graduated from Parkersburg High School and West Virginia Wesleyan College. Although his talent appeared to be primarily in baseball—he played the outfield for the Cincinnati Reds for eight years—Neale achieved pro football fame as the innovative head coach of the Philadelphia Eagles.

7. Joe Stydahar, 1912-1977 *(Shinnston, Morgantown, Beckley)*
   A star in several sports at Shinnstown High School, Joseph Lee Stydahar, a Pennsylvania native, attended Pitt briefly before transferring to West Virginia University, where he excelled in football and basketball. The Chicago Bears drafted him in 1936. Stydahar went on to become a perennial all-star tackle. Later he coached for the Los Angeles Rams, Green Bay Packers, and Chicago Cardinals. He died in Beckley in 1977.

5 Consensus Football All-Americans At West Virginia University

There have been many first-, second-, and third-team All-Americans at WVU. The following are the best of the best.

1. Ira Errett Rodgers, fullback, 1919
2. Bruce Bosley, offensive tackle, 1955
3. Darryl Talley, linebacker, 1982
4. Brian Jozwiak, tackle, 1985
5. Mike Compton, center, 1992

9 WVU Football Mountaineers Who Played in the Super Bowl

Since the Super Bowl is played in January, its date is always a year later than the football season it represents.

1. Walt Easley, fullback, San Francisco 49ers, 1981
2. Mike Fox, defensive end, New York Giants, 1991
3. David Grant, nose tackle, Cincinnati Bengals, 1989
4. Ken Herock, tight end, Oakland Raiders, 1967
5. Jeff Hostetler, quarterback, New York Giants, 1987, 1991
6. Chuck Howley, linebacker, Dallas Cowboys, 1973
7. Alvoid Mays, cornerback, Washington Redskins, 1992
8. Darryl Talley, linebacker, Buffalo Bills, 1991, 1992, 1993
9. Fulton Walker, defensive back, Miami Dolphins, 1983

7 Basketball First-team All-Americans at WVU

All-Americans are selected by various groups and publications. Several players on this list were chosen as second- or third-team members by some raters. Only Jerry West was a unanimous first-team All-American pick—for both 1959 and 1960.

1. Scotty Hamilton, 1942

    Floyd (Scotty) Hamilton was born in Grafton and played for Grafton High. WVU's first All-American cager at 6'2", he later coached at various high schools, including Welch, and at Washington and Lee University and Ohio University.

2. Leland Byrd, 1947

    A Kentucky native, Leland Byrd led the Mountaineers to a 72-15 record in 1945-48. Nicknamed "Lefty" or "Hammer" as a player, he went on to coach at Hinton High School and Glenville State College. He became athletic director at WVU.

3. Mark Workman, 1952

    Born in Charleston, 6'9" Mark Workman, a center, averaged 20.4 points per game at WVU. He played briefly in the NBA for Philadelphia and Baltimore, averaging 5.6 points per game, after which he worked as a clothing salesman in Charlotte, NC.

4. Rod Hundley, 1957

    Known as "Hot Rod," he played a flashy, Globetrotter-style game. An accomplished dribbler, passer, shooter, and defender, Charleston-born Hundley, 6'4", scored

2,180 points for WVU and led the Mountaineers to three Southern Conference titles, 1955-57. As a pro he played six years for the Minneapolis/Los Angeles Lakers.

5. Jerry West, 1959, 1960

    A native of Cabin Creek, 6'3" Jerry West played for East Bank High School, then starred for WVU, 1958-60, averaging 24.8 points and 13.3 rebounds per game for the Mountaineers. He was a U.S. Olympian cager in Rome in 1960. Joining the L.A. Lakers, he became one of the great players in the pro game, a perennial All-NBA first team choice.

6. Rod Thorn, 1962, 1963

    Son of the Princeton police chief, 6'4" Rod Thorn was a three-time All-State star at Princeton High School. For the Mountaineers (wearing Jerry West's jersey number 44) he scored 2,180 points, 1961-63. His NBA career, plagued by injuries, took him to Baltimore, Detroit, St. Louis, and Seattle.

7. Wil Robinson, 1972

    Robinson grew up in Uniontown, PA, where he led his high school team to the state championship. At WVU he scored 1,850 points, 1970-72, and was signed by the Houston Rockets. His only season of pro basketball, however, was 1974-75, playing for the Memphis Sounds of the ABA. He averaged 8.6 points per game.

11 WV High School Basketball Players With More Than 2,000 Career Points

1. Paul Popovich, 1955-1958   2,660   (Flemington)
2. Rod Thorn, 1956-1959   2,619   (Princeton)
3. Bill Maphis, 1957-60   2,504   (Romney)
4. Herbie Brooks, 1981-1984   2,498   (Mullens)
5. Don Jones, 1956-1959   2,354   (Sherrard/Wheeling)
6. Mike Carson, 1966-1969   2,269   (Sistersville)
7. Kevin Wells, 1987-1990   2,247   (Ceredo-Kenova)
8. Ron Williams, 1961-1964   2,203   (Weir/Weirton)
9. Mick Cooper, 1961-1964   2,128   (Harman)
10. Lou Mott, 1953-1956   2,117   (Pine Grove)
11. Tim Dagostine, 1982-1985   2,116   (Poca)

6 WV High School Football Players Who Scored 200 Points in a Season

These figures represent total points scored during the regular season. The modern all-games record is 309, scored by Pineville's Curt Warner in 1978.

1. Curt Warner, 1978   263   (Pineville)
2. Paul Mitchell, 1971   254   (Stoco/Coal City)
3. Robert Alexander, 1976   220   (South Charleston)
4. Dick Horton, 1946   216   (Spencer)
5. Don Grooms, 1968   212   (Cedar Grove)
6. Jeff Swisher, 1986   204   (Sistersville)

9 Eye-Popping High School Sports Records

BASKETBALL

In the Class AAA championship game of 1977, Logan rolled over Washington Irving (Clarksburg) by a score of 111-87, an NBA-like outcome, and the only 100+ total ever in championship play. Personal highs in the state:

1. Paul Popovich, 1958 (Flemington)
   On page 161 there is a list of basketball players who racked up more than 2,000 career points. Paul Popovich (who's on the list) scored 1,086 in *one season*.

2. Danny Heater, 1960 (Burnsville)
   This isn't just a West Virginia record but a national record as well. Playing for Burnsville in a game against Widen, Danny Heater poured in 135 points.

3. Christy Cooper, 1985-88 (Circleville)
   In boys' basketball the top career scorer is Paul Popovich with 2,660 points. In girls' basketball it's Christy Cooper with 3,392—an average of 36 per game.

FOOTBALL

In a game back in 1912, New Martinsville rolled over Woodsfield, Ohio, by a margin not likely to be equaled. The final score was 157-0. Personal highs in other games:

4. Randy Hendricks, 1972   Sherman (Seth)
   Against Chapmanville, with Sherman winning, 76-26, Hendricks passed for 454 yards. He completed 13 of 22 passes, 9 for touchdowns (tying a national record).

5. John Hogshead, 1975 (Nitro)
   To put this in context: The longest field goal in NFL history is 63 yards. In a game against Poca, Nitro High's John Hogshead booted a 55-yard field goal.

6. Jeff Swisher, 1986 (Sistersville)
   In a game against Frontier High of New Matamoras, Ohio, Jeff Swisher carried the ball 22 times for 448 yards (20+ yards a carry) and nine touchdowns.

BASEBALL

In 1939-41 Charleston's East Bank High School, under Coach Bill Calvert, reeled off 51 straight victories. In 1978-79 the Tygarts Valley team made a run at the record but were stopped after 37 wins.

7. Steve Johnson, 1971 (Barboursville)
   A .300 hitter is a top performer. A .400 hitter is a phenomenon. How about Steve Johnson, then, who batted .699 for the 1971 season?

8. Pete Thackston, 1976 (Huntington)
   As a sophomore pitcher, Pete Thackston turned in an 18-0 mark, with two no-hitters and 211 strikeouts in 129 innings. He won all six tournament games for his team.

9. Andy Wakefield, 1977 (Beckley)
   Move over Dale Long, Don Mattingly, and Ken Griffey, Jr., each of whom hit homers in eight straight major league games. In 1977 Beckley's Andy Wakefield connected for home runs in nine consecutive games.

3 Great Rivers for Whitewater Rafting

Whitewater abounds in West Virginia. More than 2,000 miles of streams plunge through the Appalachians, providing plenty of runs for thrill-seekers, from novices to experts. About 200 miles of the state's rivers have been designated for commercial rafting, and a number of outfitters offer professional guides on the three rivers listed below as well as on the Tygart, Greenbrier, Bluestone, South Branch (Potomac), Meadow, Shenandoah, and Big Sandy Creek. For information, phone WVPRO (304) 346-4660, or the West Virginia Division of Tourism & Parks (800) CALL-WVA.

1. New River

    The New River is popular with rafters from novices to experts. Rapids are classed from I to V (the Class VI ranking means "nearly impossible"). Trips are available from April to October. The upper New is fairly easy, but the lower New, through the New River Gorge, escalates from Class II to Class V.

2. Cheat River

    Supposedly named because it "cheated" some early travelers of their lives, the Cheat River is a challenge for intermediate to advanced rafters. The rapids of the "wild Cheat" are classed from III to V+.

3. Gauley River

    One of the two greatest whitewater rivers in the United States (and seventh among the rivers of the world) the Gauley has 50 major rapids out of a total of 100 in an exciting 38-mile stretch. Some outfitters take two days to run it, with camping overnight on the riverbank.

6 West Virginia Ski Resorts

Four of these resorts feature alpine (downhill) skiing, while four have nordic (crosscountry) skiing. Yes, that's eight, not six. Two resorts—Canaan Valley and Timberline—offer both.

1. WinterPlace
   Seventeen miles south of Beckley off I-77, WinterPlace has 24 slopes with a maximum vertical drop of 603 feet. (304) 787-3221.

2. Elk River
   Near Slatyfork on U.S. 219, Elk Creek offers nordic skiiing day and night. (304) 572-3771.

3. Snowshoe/Silver Creek
   Near Slatyfork on U.S. 219, Snowshoe/Silver Creek is West Virginia's largest ski resort, with 50 slopes and a maximum vertical drop of 1,500 feet. (304) 572-1000.

4. White Grass
   This, the first of four ski areas near Davis, has 50 km of maintained cross-country terrain. (304) 866-4114.

5. Canaan Valley
   At Canaan Valley Resort State Park, West Virginia's first ski resort, there are 33 slopes with a maximum vertical drop of 850 feet. (304) 866-4121.

6. Timberline
   Near Davis, Timberline has 25 trails and a 1,084-foot maximum vertical drop. Its longest run is two miles. (304) 866-4801.

Pipestem Resort State Park, like many of the state parks, offers a variety of outdoor activities—here, fishing and paddleboating.

35 West Virginia Fishing Records

This list, based on weight, not length, is a simplified version of the one prepared by the Wildlife Resources Section of the West Virginia Division of Natural Resources. Weights (in pounds) are rounded off to the nearest tenth. [Counties are shown in brackets.]

Species	Weight	Where Caught	Year
1. Largemouth bass	10.8	Sleepy Creek Lake	1979
2. Smallmouth bass	9.8	South Branch, Potomac	1971
3. Rock bass	1.8	Big Sandy Creek	1964
4. Spotted bass	3.8	R. D. Bailey Lake	1988
5. Striped bass	21.0	New River	1981
6. Hybrid striped bass	16.8	Kanawha River	1985
7. White bass	4.6	New River	1985
8. Bluegill	2.8	Pond [Randolph]	1986
9. Bowfin	7.4	Pond [Berkeley]	1981
10. Buffalo	38.0	Little Kanawha River	1976
11. Carp	44.0	Tygart River	1989
12. Bullhead catfish	6.1	Tygart Lake headwaters	1977
13. Channel catfish	27.1	Private lake [Grant]	1991
14. Flathead catfish	70.0	Little Kanawha River	1956
15. Chain pickerel	4.8	Fort Ashby Lake	1978
16. Crappie	4.1	Meathouse Fork	1971
17. Eel	7.3	Bunker Hill Quarry	1977
18. Fallfish	3.5	North Fork, South Branch	1970
19. Freshwater drum	27.0	South Fork, Hughes River	1989
20. Longnose gar	17.5	Elk River	1975
21. Goldeye	3.0	Ohio River	1983
22. Muskellunge	43.0	Elk River	1955
23. Northern pike	22.1	Dog Run Lake	1989

Species (cont.)	Weight	Where Caught	Year
24. Paddlefish	70.0	Little Kanawha River	1965
25. Sauger	4.7	Ohio River	1985
26. Skipjack	2.4	Kanawha River	1988
27. Sturgeon	12.5	Ohio River	1949
28. Tiger musky	28.1	Sleep Creek [Morgan]	1991
29. Brook trout	6.5	Stoney Creek	1981
30. Brown trout	16.0	South Branch, Potomac	1968
31. Golden rainbow trout	8.6	Stonecoal Lake	1987
32. Rainbow trout	11.5	South Branch, Potomac	1991
33. Tiger trout	6.7	Greenbrier River	1986
34. Walleye	17.2	Gauley River	1990
35. Yellow perch	1.8	Tygart Lake	1985

Sources

This is a list of books consulted in compiling *The West Virginia Book of Lists*. Only books are included here, not magazines, newspapers, brochures, or other sources that provided some of the lists or items within the lists. Special mention should be made, however, of *Wonderful West Virginia*, *Goldenseal*, and the Bicentennial Special of *The West Virginia Hillbilly*, which proved exceptionally helpful.

Barron's Profiles of American Colleges, 19th ed. New York: Barron's, 1992.
Barth, Jack. *Roadside Hollywood*. Chicago. Contemporary Books, 1990.
Barzun, Jacques, and Wendell Hertig Taylor, *A Catalogue of Crime*, rev. ed. New York: Harper & Row, 1989.
The Baseball Encyclopedia, 9th ed. New York: Macmillan, 1993.
Boatner, Mark Mayo III. *The Civil War Dictionary*. New York: David McKay, 1959.
Bragg, George, and Melody Bragg. *West Virginia Unsolved Murders*. Glen Jean: GEM Publications, 1992.
Bricktop, with James Haskins. *Bricktop*. New York: Atheneum, 1983.
Cherniack, Martin. *The Hawk's Nest Incident: America's Worst Industrial Disaster*. New Haven, CT: Yale University Press, 1986.
Clarke, Donald, ed. *The Penguin Encyclopedia of Popular Music*. New York: Viking, 1989.
The College Handbook, 1994. New York: College Entrance Examination Board, 1994.
Comstock, Jim. *West Virginia Heritage Encyclopedia* and *Supplements*. Richwood: Jim Comstock, 1974-76.
Comstock, Jim. *West Virginia Women*. Richwood: Jim Comstock, 1974.
Conte, Robert S. *The History of the Greenbrier: America's Resort*. Charleston: Pictorial Histories Publishing Co., 1989.

Donnelly, Shirley. *Yesterday and Today: Historical Highlights of Southern West Virginia (A Keepsake I, II, III)*. [Fayetteville]: Fayetteville County Historical Society, [n.d.].

Fetherling, Dale. *Mother Jones: The Miners' Angel*. Carbondale: Southern Illinois University Press, 1974.

Halliwell, Leslie. *Halliwell's Filmgoer's and Video Viewer's Companion*, 9th ed. New York: Harper & Row, 1988.

Harris, William H., and Judith S. Levey, eds. *The New Columbia Encyclopedia*. New York: Columbia University Press, 1975.

Holmes, Darrell E., ed. *West Virginia Blue Book, 1991*. Beckley: BJW Printing and Office Supplies, 1991.

Johnson, Lloyd, and Miles Wolff, eds. *The Encyclopedia of Minor League Baseball*. Durham, NC: Baseball America, 1993.

James, Bessie Rowland. *Anne Royall's U.S.A*. New Brunswick, NJ: Rutgers University Press, 1972.

Keys, Kevin, ed. *West Virginia Basketball, 1992-93*. Morgantown: WVU Sports Communications Office, [1992].

Keys, Kevin, ed. *West Virginia Football Guide, 1993*. Morgantown: WVU Department of Intercollegiate Athletics, [1993].

Lanier, Pamela. *The Complete Guide to Bed & Breakfasts, Inns & Guesthouses in the United States and Canada*. Oakland, CA: Lanier Publishing Co., 1992.

Lord, Suzanne, and Jon Metzger. *The West Virginia One-Day Trip Book*. McLean, VA: EPM Publications, 1993.

Malone, Bill C. *Country Music, U.S.A.*, rev. ed. Austin: University of Texas Press, 1985.

Maltin, Leonard. *TV Movies and Video Guide*, 1994 ed. New York: Signet, 1994.

Mendell, Ronald L. *Who's Who in Basketball*. New Rochelle, NY: Arlington House, 1973.

Morgan, John G. *West Virginia Governors: 1863-1980*. Charleston: Charleston Newspapers, 1981.

Nash, Jay Robert. *Bloodletters and Badmen*. 3 vols. New York: Warner Books, 1973, 1975.

Neft, David S., and Richard M. Cohen, eds. *The Football Encyclopedia: The Complete History of NFL Football from 1892 to the Present.* New York: St. Martin's Press, 1991.

1992 Harris West Virginia Manufacturing Directory. Twinsburg, OH: Harris Publishing, 1992.

1994 Mobil Travel Guide: Middle Atlantic. New York: Prentice Hall, 1994.

Notable American Women, 1607-1950: A Biographical Dictionary. Cambridge, MA: Harvard University Press, 1971.

Nugent, Tom. *Death at Buffalo Creek: The 1972 West Virginia Flood Disaster.* New York: W. W. Norton, 1973.

The Official National Football League Record and Fact Book. New York: Workman, 1992.

Porter, David L., ed. *Biographical Dictionary of American Sports: Football.* Westport, CT: Greenwood Press, 1987.

Porter, David L., ed. *Biographical Dictionary of American Sports: Outdoor Sports.* Westport, CT: Greenwood Press, 1988.

Raft West Virginia. Elkins: Communication by Design, 1994.

Ragan, David. *Who's Who in Hollywood.* New York: Facts on File, 1992.

Rice, Otis K. *West Virginia: A History.* Lexington: University of Kentucky Press, 1985.

Ski West Virginia. Elkins: The Pegasus Group, 1993.

Stambler, Irwin, and Grelun Landon. *The Encyclopedia of Folk, Country & Western Music.* New York: St. Martin's, 1983.

Stetler, Susan L., ed. *Almanac of Famous People,* 4th ed. 3 vols. Detroit: Gale Research, 1989.

Teets, Bob, and Shelby Young. *Killing Waters I* and *II.* Terra Alta, 1985.

Van Doren, Charles, ed. *Webster's American Biographies.* Springfield, MA: G&C Merriam Co., 1974.

Waller, Altina L. *Feud: Hatfields, McCoys, and Social Change in Appalachia, 1860-1900.* Chapel Hill: University of North Carolina Press, 1988.

West Virginia, It's You! A Complete Guide to West Virginia.
    n.p.: Donald J. Molter [1993]
Who Was Who in America, 10 vols. Chicago/Providence, NJ:
    Marquis Who's Who, 1963-93.
Wilkerson, Ellen S. and Ann W. Stowers. *Adventures in West
    Virginia: Day Trips and Longer Travels*. Huntingston:
    Aegina Press, 1988.
Williams, John Alexander. *West Virginia: A History*. New York:
    W. W. Norton, 1984.
Williams, John Alexander. *West Virginia: A History for Beginners*.
    Charleston: Appalachian Editions, 1993.
The World Almanac and Book of Facts, 1994. New York: Pharos
    Books, 1994.
Writers' Program of the Work Projects Administration. *West
    Virginia: A Guide to the Mountain State*. New York:
    Oxford University Press, 1941.
W. Va. High School Yearbook, 1992-93. Parkersburg: Secondary
    School Activities Commission, [1993].

Index

Abie's Irish Rose, 25
"Act of God, An," 144
Ada, 59
Adams, John, 15
Ada's Club, Parkersburg, 88
African American Baptists
African Zion Baptist Church, 113
Air Force C-47 crash, 84
Air National Guard, 84
airplane industry, 122-23
Alderson, 19
Alexander Campbell Mansion, 111
Alex Driving South, 28
Alice, 57
Allen, George, 32
All Fall Down, 31
All the Brave Promises, 27
All the King's Men, 25
Alma, 57
alternate-use buildings, 116
Altman, Robert, 25
American Scene, 143
Ames garden tools, 120
Amherst Industries, 96
Andrews Methodist Episcopal Church, 114
Andrew S. Rowan Memorial Home for the Aged, 134
Andy Griffith Show, The, 25
Anglin's Ford, 64
Annott, Robert, 107
Ansted, 72, 75
Anthony, 57
Anthony, Tony, 26
Antioch, 16
Apollo Civic Theatre, 149
Appalachian League, 151, 154-55
Appalachian Power Company, 120
Arnoldsville, 54
Arthur, 57
Arthurdale, 67, 70
Art Museum, Charleston, 117
Ashford General Hospital, 138
Asian-American population, WV rank, 98
Assurance, 62

A. T. Gift Winery, 131
Athens, 61
Atkinson, George W., 45
Audra State Park, 74
Aurora, 75
Averell, W. W., 79
axe factory, world's largest, 96
Azulay, Judy, 23

B & O Railroad, 41, 86, 94, 121
Babcock State Park, 73
Back Fork, Elk River, 95, 108
Bailes Brothers, 22
Bailey, Pearl, 22
Bailey murders, Parkersburg, 87-88
Baker, Newton D., 43
Baker, R. H., 105
bald eagle, 109
Bald Knob, 70, 71
Baltimore Bullets, 34
Baltimore Orioles, 154-55
Barberton, OH, High School, 32
Barbour County, 51, 61
Barboursville, 73, 163
Barron, W. W., 47
Barth, Jack, 142
Bartley, 81
baseball, WV rank, 97
Baseball Hall of Fame, 152-53
Bass, fishing records, 167
Bath, 14, 71, 94
Batten, William, 37
Battle Creek, MI, 37
Battle of Blair Mountain, 28, 86-87
Battles, Cliff, 156, 157
Bavarian Inn and Lodge, 131
Baylor, Don, 155
Beartown State Park, 75
Beatrice, 57
Beaver, 74
Beckley, 26, 47, 50, 55, 60, 118, 140, 148, 157, 163, 165
bed & breakfasts, 128-29
Bee, Clair, 34
Beech Fork Lake, 107
Beech Fork State Park, 73

Beech Mountain (railroad), 121
Belle, 57
Belle Boyd in Camp and Prison, 16
Benedict, Pinckney, 30, 144
Benedum, Michael Late, 36
Benedum Trees Oil Co., 36
Benwood, 80
Berdine's Variety Store, 127
Berkeley Castle, 112
Berkeley County, 50, 53, 55, 61, 167
Berkeley Springs, 14, 31, 51, 71, 73, 75, 94, 112, 128, 133, 135
Berkeley Springs State Park, 71, 75, 133
Berlin, 61
Berry Leon (Chu), 22
Bethany, 111, 113, 115
Bethany College, 111, 113, 115
Bethlehem Steel Corp., 123
Beury, 69
Beverly, 56, 57, 67, 78
Biarritz, France 19
"Bicentennial Salute," 123
bicycle riding, WV rank, 97
Big Bend Tunnel, 19
Big Dipper roller coaster, 99
Big Isaac, 60
"Big Moses," 96
Big Sandy Creek, 164, 167
Big Sandy River, 60, 102
Big Trouble, 25
"billion-dollar coal field," 58
Bim, 59
Bird, Walter, 112
births, WV rank, 98
Bishop, Michael, 88
Black for Remembrance, 31
Black Hotel, 39
Blackwater Falls State Park, 74
"Blair Morgan"trilogy, 28
Blair Mountain, 87
Blenko Glass Company, 125
Blennerhassett, Harman, 111
Blennerhassett, Margaret, 111
Blennerhassett Historical State Park, 74
Blennerhassett Hotel, 137
Blennerhassett Island, 14, 111
Blenerhassett Mansion, 111
Blindman, 26
Blind Spring Ramble, 31
Blizzard, "General" Bill, 87
Blood Tie, 27
Bluefield, 22, 28, 55, 65, 88, 139, 140, 154-55
Bluefield Daily Telegraph, 140
Bluefield Orioles, 154-55
Bluefield State College, 88
bluegill, fishing record, 167
Blue Jacket (Marmaduke Van Swearingen), 18
Blue Ridge League, 152
Blue Ridge Mountains, 66, 85
Bluestone Lake, 107
Bluestone Scenic National River, 75, 108, 164
Bluestone State Park, 74
Blue Sulphur Springs, 134
boatbuilding industry, 122
Boddicker, Mike, 155
Boise, Thomas, 39
Boley and McKee stories, 31
Bolivar, 23, 56
Bolt, 21
Boone, Daniel, 14
Boone County, 51, 53, 57, 58, 59, 60, 61, 62
Boreman, Arthur I., 45
Bosley, Bruce, 158
bowling, WV rank, 97
Boyd, Belle, 16
Boyle, W. A. (Tony), 37
Bradshaw, 56
Braids, 24
Bramwell, 65, 74
Braxton County, 51, 54, 59
"Break in the Film, A," 30
Brett, George, 33
bricks, first used for paving, 94
Bricktop, 18, 19
Bridge Day, 90
Bridgeport, 36, 132

INDEX • 175

Bright Morning, 128-29
Brinkley, David, 104
Broadway Open House, 25
Brooke County, 20, 51, 52, 63
Brooke Glass Company, 125
Brooks, Herbie, 161
Brooksville, 54
Brown, T. Bailey, 94
Brown, Drollene, 29
Brown, Jim, 26
Brown, John, 14, 15, 66, 82, 83, 118, 135
Bruceton Mills, 76
Bryan, William Jennings, 41
Buck, Pearl S., 16
Buckhannon, 28, 29, 51, 65, 74, 115, 156, 157
Buckhannon River, 108
Buckley, Kate, 29
Bud, 59
Buffalo, 41
buffalo, fishing record, 167
Buffalo Creek, 84, 85
Buffalo Creek & Gauley (railroad), 121
Buffalo Mining Company, 85
Bunker Hill Quarry, 167
Burdette, Lew, 32
Burial mound, largest, 95
Burkett, Jesse (The Crab), 32, 33
Burnsville, 162
Burnsville Lake, 107
Burr, Aaron, 14, 111
Burton, 39
"Busby's Rat," 145
Byars, Betsy, 29
Byrd, Harry Flood, 42
Byrd, Leland, 159
Byrd, Robert C., 42

C & O Railway, 19, 49, 69, 70, 72, 116, 121
Cabell County, 20, 50, 53, 55, 57, 59
Cabin Creek, 33, 86, 160
Cabot, Inc., 123
Cabwaylingo State Forest, 76
Cacapon Resort State Park, 73

Cacapon River, 108
Cairo, 61, 74
Calcutta, 61
Caldwell, 72, 76
Calhoun, John C., 53, 54, 134
Calhoun County, 52, 53, 54, 57, 59
Calloway, Cab, 22
Calvert, Bill, 163
Calvin, 57
Calvin Price State Forest, 76
Camden, Johnson N., 35
Camden Consolidated Oil Co., 35
Camden Park, 99
Cameo Glass, 126
Campbell, Alexander, 111, 113, 115
Campbell's Creek, 14
Camp Creek, 74, 76
Camp Creek State Forest, 76
Camp Creek State Park, 74
camping, WV rank, 97
Canaan Valley Resort State Park, 71, 73, 136, 165
Caperton, Gaston N., 48
Capitol Complex, Charleston, 46, 112, 117
Capitol Music Hall, 147
Capon Bridge, 89
Capon Springs, 47, 135
Carmichaels, 35
Carnifex Ferry, Battle of, 78
Carnifex Ferry Battlefield State Park, 75
carp, fishing record, 167
Carrick's Ford, Battle of, 78
Carry On, Mr. Bowditch, 29
Carson, Mike, 161
Carter, Jimmy, 42, 44
Casavant organ, 115
Casey, Bernie, 26
Cass, 70, 71, 72, 74
Cassavetes, John, 25
Cass Scenic Railroad State Park, 70, 71, 74
catfish, fishing records, 167
Cathedral State Park, 75
Cedar Creek State Park, 73

Cedar Grove, 161
Cedar Lakes, 92
Central League, 152
Ceredo, 126, 161
Ceredo-Kenova High School, 161
Chafin, Don, 87
chain pickerel, fishing record, 167
Chapmanville, 162
Charleston, 17, 21, 22, 26, 27, 32, 33,
    40, 44, 48, 50, 55, 63, 64, 76, 84,
    89, 91, 94, 95, 96, 99, 111, 112,
    113, 117, 140, 141, 145, 146,
    147, 148, 159, 163
Charleston Area Medical Center, 120
Charleston Ballet, 147
Charleston Daily Mail, 140, 141
Charleston Gazette, The, 140, 141
Charleston Light Opera Company, 148
Charleston Municipal Auditorium, 147
Charles Town, 14, 50, 63, 66, 82, 83,
    91, 92, 94, 114, 128, 149
Chasnoff, Joe, 23
Cheat Mountain, Battle of, 15, 78
Cheat River, 78, 102, 164
Chenoweth, Eli and Lemuel, 105
Cherniack, Martin, 149
Cherry River, 102
Cherry Tree Bottoms, 64
Chesapeake and Potomac, 120
Chesimard, Joanne, 100
Chessie System, 123
Chicago "Black Sox," 34
Chicago Tribune, 143
Chief Logan State Park, 73
Children's Farm, Wheeling, 99
Children's Museum, Charleston, 117
Chilton House, 130
Chloe, 24, 57
Church, Sam, 38
Church, Ellen, 39
Cincinnati Reds, 34, 151
Circleville, 162
Civic Center Theater, Charleston, 147
Clarksburg, 13, 15, 23, 25, 26, 27, 28,
    30, 31, 36, 39, 40, 42, 43, 44, 50,
    55, 60, 90, 131, 140, 141, 162

Clarksburg Exponent, The, 140, 141
Clay, 52, 91
Clay, Henry, 53, 54, 134, 137
Clay County, 52, 53, 54, 57, 59, 61,
    91, 95
Clay County Ramp Dinner, 91
Clear Creek, 22
Clendenin, George, 63
Clendenin's Settlement, 63, 64
Clendenin's Station, 63
Cleveland, Grover, 43
Cleveland Spiders, 32
Cliffside Amphitheatre, 148
Clifftop, 73
Cline, Patsy, 21, 142
clothespin factory, world's largest, 122
Cloyd's Mountain, Battle of, 20
Coalbottom, 58
Coalburg, 58
Coal City, 58, 161
Coaldale, 58
Coalfield, 58
Coal Fork, 58
Coal House, Williamson, 68
Coal Mountain, 58
Coal River, 102
Coalton, 58
Coalwood, 58
"Coin" Harvey, 41
Coin's Financial School, 41
Colesquo (Cornstalk), 18
Colliers, 131
Collins, Bonnie, 29
Columbia Gas System, 123
Comfort, 62
Communists in government, 83
Compton, Mike, 158
Confidence, 62
Congressional Quarterly, 97, 98
Conley, William G., 47
Conlin, Thomas, 147
Conrail, 121
Consolidation Coal Co., 36, 120, 123
Consol No. 9 Mine, 81
Continental Oil Co., 123
Coolidge, Calvin, 41, 44

Cooney, Nancy Evans, 29
Cooper, Christy, 162
Cooper, Mick, 161
Cooper, Stoney, 21
Cooper, Wilma Lee, 21
Coopers Rock State Forest, 76, 101
Copas, Cowboy, 21
Cornbread, Earl and Me, 26
Corningware, 120
Cornstalk (Colesquo), 18
Cornwell, John J., 47
Corridor "L," 104
Cottonwood Inn, 128
cougar, 110
covered bridges, 104-06
C. P. Huntington (sternwheeler), 99
Craik, James, 111
Craik-Patton House, 111
Cranberry Glass, 126
Cranbury River, 102
crappie, fishing record, 167
crimes, WV rank, 98
Crosman, Henrietta, 25
Cross Lanes, 22, 55
"Cross of Gold" speech, 41
Crum, 60
CSX, 121, 123
Cucumber, 60
Cultural Center, Charleston, 23, 117
Cuppytown, 64
Currey, Richard, 28
Curtin, Phyllis, 23
Cyclone, 62

Dagmar, 25
Dagostine, Tim, 161
Dalzell-Viking, 125
Dan, 59
Dark Mountains, The, 27
Davis, 41, 71, 73, 74, 75, 128, 165
Davis, Glenn, 32
Davis, Henry Gassaway, 35, 41, 112
Davis, John W., 42
Davis and Elkins College, 90, 112
Davy, 57, 68
Day Christ Died, The, 26

DC-9 crash, 85
DDT, 109
Dean firearms collection, 117
Death at Buffalo Creek, 149
Deem, Abram, 39
Deep Water, 102
Deer Creek Valley, 100
Delahanty, Ed, 152
Dents Run Covered Bridge, 106
Denver, John, 141
DeWitt, Joyce, 26
diabetes, deaths due to, 97
diamond, largest alluvial, 96
Diamond, Legs, 18
Dickens, Little Jimmy, 21
Dicterow, Glenn, 147
Didi: A Love Story, 30
Dillard, Annie, 144
Dingess, 47
Disciples of Christ, 113, 115
Doddridge County, 52, 59, 60, 62
Dog Day Afternoon, 26
Dog Run Lake, 167
Dogs of God, 30, 144
Dogwood Gap, 78
Doll's Gap, 16
Dominion Post, Morgantown, 140
Don, 59
Dooley, Paul, 25
Dorothy, 57
Douglas, John, 31
Dourif, Brad, 26
Droop, 60
Droop Mountain, 79, 88
Droop Mountain, Battle of, 20, 79
Droop Mountain Battlefield State Park, 75
Dru, Joanne, 25
drum, freshwater, fishing record, 167
dulcimers, 24
Duliere, Warren, 89
Dulty, George,
Dunbar, 55
Dun Glen Hotel, 69
Dunlow, 76
Dunmore, 76

Dunn Country Inn, 129
Duo, 59
"Dust on the Bible," 22
Duval, Isaac H., 20

Eagle fuel cans, 120
Easley, Walt, 158
East Bank High School, Charleston, 33, 160, 163
Eastern Associated Coal Corp., 120
Eastern cougar, 110
Eastern Gas and Fuel Associates, 123
East Huntington bridge, 104
East Lynn Lake, 107
Eby, 59
Eccles, 80
Echols, 20, 79
Eden Tree, The, 27
Edna Gas, 32, 156
eel, fishing record, 167
Egnor, Virginia Ruth (Dagmar), 25
Ehlerman, Joe and Karen, 23
E. I. Dupont De Nemours & Co., 120
Eisenhower, Dwight D., 44
Eleanor, 57, 67
Eliot, T. S., 19
Elizabeth, 52, 57
Elk, 59
Elkins, 41, 43, 47, 51, 55, 67, 90, 91, 112, 129, 140
Elkins, Davis, 36
Elkins, Stephen B., 35, 43, 112
Elk River, 95, 102, 167
Elk River (ski resort), 165
Elk River Inn (Gassaway), 132
Elk River Inn, The, (Slatyfork), 129
Elk Valley (railroad), 121
Elkview, 24
Elkwater, 15, 78
Ellenboro, 56, 126
Ellery Queen's Mystery Magazine, 31
Elm Grove, 111
Entler Hotel, Shepherdstown, 66
Ernie's Esquire, 130
Esso, 37
Ethel, 57

Eva, 59
Everettsville, 34, 80
Explosive Plant C, Nitro, 67

Fairchild FH-227 crash, 85
Fairfax Stone Historic Monument, 75
Fairmont, 27, 33, 36, 45, 50 55, 74, 75, 130, 140
Fairview, 33
Fallen Timbers, Battle of, 18
fallfish, fishing record, 167
Fall Mountain Heritage Arts & Crafts Festival, 92
fanshell, 110
Far, 59
Farmington, 32, 81, 156
Farnsworth, Daniel D. T., 45
Fatal Light, 28
Fayette County, 50, 57, 58, 59, 62, 69, 70, 80, 81, 108, 124, 156
Fayetteville, 50, 90, 96, 104
Feast of the Ramson, 90-91
Federal Prison Camp, 99-100
Felts, Albert, 86-87
Fenton Art Glass Factory and Museum, 125
Ferrell, Conchata, 26
Festival of Lights, Wheeling, 72
Fetherling, Dale, 17, 149
Fetterman, 94
Fiddle and Banjo Contest, 90
Fife, Barney, 25
Fink, Mike, 18
First Presbyterian Church, Charleston, 113
Fisher, Suzanne, 23
Fisher Ridge Wines, 131
fishing, 166
fishing records, 167-68
Flatwoods, 23
Fleming, A. Brooks, 45
Flemington, 32, 161, 162
Flesherville, 64
Floe, 24
Floyd, John B., 78
flying squirrel, 110

INDEX • 179

Fokker Trimotors, 122
Folger, Abigail, 40
Follansbee, 34, 153
"For a Coffin of Pine," 31
Ford, Gerald R., 40
Ford, Henry, 70, 123
Fork Lick, 64
Forksburg, 47
Forks of Cheat Winery, 131
Forks-of-Coal, 58
Forrestal, James, 44
Fort Ashby Lake, 167
Fort Henry, 17
Fort Lee, 63
Fort Union, 64
4-H Camp, first, 95
Four Minute Lunch, 40
Fox, Mike, 158
Frankford, 45
Franklin, 52, 56, 120
fraternity slaying, Bluefield, 88
French and Indian War, 94
freshwater mussel, 110
Frey, Jim, 155
From the Heart, 22
Frost, 62
Fry, 59
Fry, Birkett D., 20
Frye, Henry, 135

Gandeevile, 24
Gap Mills, 19, 74
gar, longnose, fishing record, 167
Gardner, Julia, 137
Garnett, Robert S., 78
Gary, 57, 68
gasoline tax, first, 95
Gassaway, 41
gas well, world's greatest, 96
Gatski, Frank, 32, 156
Gauley Bridge, 84
Gauley River, 102, 108, 164, 168
Gauley River National Recreation
   Area, 75
Gay, 59
Gem, 59

"General" (horse), 117
General Adam Stephen House, 111
General Lewis Inn, 132
Geneva, 61
Gentile Glass Company, 125
Georgia Pacific Corp., 123
Germany Valley, 103
Ghent, 61
Giardina, Denise, 28, 139, 144
Gilbert, 57
Gilbert, Cass, 46, 99
Gilmer County, 52, 54, 57, 60
Glasgow, 61
Glasscock, William E., 45
Glass Swan, The, 126
Glen, 57
Glen Dale, 33, 122
Glenville, 52, 60, 73
"God's Acre," 111
Goff, Nathan, Jr., 43
Golden Delicious apple, 54, 95
Goldenseal, 145-46
goldeye, fishing record, 167
golf, WV rank, 97
Good, Jim, 24
Good Children's Zoo, 99
Good Earth, The, 118
Goodwill, 62
Gordimer, Nadine, 28, 143
Gore, Howard M., 44, 47
Governor's Mansion, 112
Grace, 57
Grafton, 34, 51, 74, 78, 95, 114, 157,
   159
"Grand Ballroom," 103
Grandview Park, Beckley, 148
Grant, David, 158
Grant, Ulysses S., 53
Grant County, 51, 53, 57, 62, 76, 167
Grantsville, 52
Grave Creek Mound State Park, 75, 95
gray bat, 110
Gray Sulphur Springs, 134
Green Bank, 71, 93, 100
Greenbrier, The, 65, 100, 130, 133,
   137-38

Greenbrier County, 50, 52, 53, 57, 59, 60, 65, 76, 135
Greenbrier Course, The, 138
Greenbrier River, 85, 102, 108, 164, 168
Greenbrier River Trail, 72, 74
Greenbrier State Forest, 76
Greenbrier Valley Theatre, 148
Green Hill Cemetery, Union, 65
Green Sulphur Springs, 134
Gregg, William
Greer, Hal, 32
Grey, Zane, 17
Grimm, David L., 88
Grogan, Daniel, 39
Grooms, Don, 161
Grove, 47
Grove, Lefty, 152
Grubb, Davis, 27, 30, 143, 145
Guggenheim family, 80
Guyandotte, 64
Guyandotte River, 102
Gypsy, 60

Hacker Valley, 73
Hale, Willie, 88
Halliehurst, 112
Hamilton, Alexander, 14
Hamilton, Scotty, 159
Hamlin, 15, 51, 95
Hamon Glass Studio, 126
Hampshire County, 51, 59
Hampshire House, 129
Hampton Institute, VA, 15
Hancock County, 40, 52, 55, 61
Hanks, Nancy, 16
Hanover shoes, 120
Hardy County, 51, 53, 57, 59, 109, 135
Hare Krishna murder, 89
Harman, 161
harperella, 108
Harpers Ferry, 14, 15, 23, 45, 64, 66, 83, 94, 98, 128, 131, 135, 142
Harpers Ferry Arsenal, 82
Harpers Ferry National Historical Park, 118

Harper's Old Country Store, 126
Harris, Thomas M., 20
Harrison, Benjamin, 43, 134
Harrison County, 44, 47, 50, 53, 55, 60
Harris Riverfront Park, 147
Harrisville, 51, 127
Harshman, Marc, 29
Hart, Nancy, 16
Harvey, 57
Harvey, W. H. (Coin), 41
Hatfield, "Devil Anse," 83
Hatfield, Henry D., 47
Hatfield, Sid, 87
Hatfield-McCoy feud, 83
Hawkins, Harold (Hawkshaw), 21
Hawks Nest Incident, The, 149
Hawks Nest State Park, 72, 75
Hawks Nest Tunnel, 84
Hayes, Rutherford B., 43
heart disease, deaths from, 97
Heartland, 26
Heater, Danny, 162
Heaven's Gate, 26
Hedgesville, 136
Helvetia, 65-66
Hemingway, Ernest, 19
Henderson, Oral, 24
Henderson Hall, 112
Hendricks, Randy, 162
Henry, 41, 57
Henry, John, 18, 19, 118
Herald-Dispatch, Huntington, 140
Heritage Station, 116
Herock, Ken, 158
Hickman, Ann, 24
Highcoal, 58
highest point in WV, 98
highest temperature in WV, 98
highest WV county, 98
Highlawn Inn, 128
"Hillbilly Fever," 21
Hillbrook Inn, 128
Hillsboro, 16, 75, 107, 118
Hinton, 51, 74, 80, 130, 159
Hispanic population, WV rank, 98
Historic Hotels of America, 137

INDEX • 181

Hix, 59
Hoffmann, William, 27
Hogshead, John, 163
Holden, 68
Hole, The, 64
Holly River State Park, 73
Hollywood Squares, The, 25
Holt, Homer A. (Rocky), 47
Holtz, Louis (Lou), 34
homes, sales of, WV rank, 97
Horton, Dick, 161
Hostetler, Jeff, 158
Hotcoal, 58
Hot Springs, 134
Houser, David, 24
Howley, Chuck, 158
Hoy, 59
Hubbard, Elbert, 19
Huff, Sam, 32, 156
Hundley, Rod, 32, 159-60
Hunnicutt Field, Princeton, 151
hunting, WV rank, 97
Huntington, 21, 22, 25, 26, 30, 32, 41, 50, 55, 64, 84, 85, 99, 116, 117, 130, 140, 147, 153, 156, 163
Huntington Chamber Orchestra, 147
Huntington Museum of Art, 117, 147
Huntley, Chet, 104
Huntley-Brinkley Bridge, 104
Hur, 59
Hurley, Jay, 127
Hurricane, 56, 62
Hurricane Juan, 85
Huttonsville, 76

Iager, 96
"I'm Little but I'm Loud," 21
Indiana bat, 109
Indian Creek covered bridge, 105
Innocents, The, 27
Intelligencer, The, Wheeling, 140, 141
Inter-Mountain, The, Elkins, 140
International Mother's Day shrine, 114
International Ramp and Augusta Dulcimer Festival, 91
Ira, 59

Isbin, Sharon, 147
Italian Heritage Festival, 90
Itmann, 68
Ivy, 59
"I Wasted a Nickel," 21

Jackson, Andrew, 53
Jackson, Jacob B., 45
Jackson, Thomas J. (Stonewall), 13, 15, 20
Jackson County, 51, 53, 57, 59, 60
Jackson's Mill, 92
Jacob, John J., 45
James River, 110
James spinymussel, 110
Jane Lew, 94, 126
Jarvis, Anna, 114
J. C. Penney Co., 37
Jed, 81
Jed Coal and Coke Company, 81
Jefferson, Thomas, 53, 134, 144
Jefferson County, 50, 53, 66, 98
Jefferson County Chamber of Commerce, 92
Jenkins, Albert Gallatin, 20
Jenkins Randolph Lake, 107
Jesse, 57
Jim Reid's, 131
Job, 59
John Brown's Fort, 82
Johnson, Louis A., 44
Johnson, Steve, 163
Jones, Don, 161
Jones, Grover, 96
Jones, Mary (Mother), 17, 86
Jones, "Punch," 96
"Josephine Ford" (airplane), 123
Josephs Mills, 47
Joy, 59, 62
Jozwiak, Brian, 158
JSC Auditorium, 147
Juilliard School of Music, 23
Justice, 62

Kanauga, OH, 85
Kanawha Airport, 84

Kanawha County, 14, 20, 45, 50, 52, 53, 54, 55, 57, 58, 59, 61, 62, 63, 67
Kanawha field (coal), 86
Kanawha Players, 148
Kanawha River, 14, 102, 167, 168
Kanawha State Forest, 76
Kanawha Valley, 94, 122
Kansas City Royals, 33
Kelley's Creek & Northwestern, 121
Kellogg Co., 37
Kennedy, John F., 44
Kenova, 161
Kermit, 57
Keyser, 42, 51, 64, 131, 140
Killarney, 61
Kingsford charcoal briquets, 120
Kingwood, 47, 51, 56
Kirkwood Limited, 131
Kirtanananda Swami Bhaktipada, 89
Kmart Corporation, 120
Knife in My Hands, The, 143
Knotts, Don, 25
Knowles, John, 27
Kroger Co., The, 120
Kruk, John, 32
Kuhn, Loeb & Company, 44
Ku Klux Klan, 89
Kumbrabow State Forest, 76
Kump, H. Guy, 47

Lahti, Keith, 24
Lake, Steve, 155
Lakeview Theatre, 149
Ladies Garland, 94
Landmark Studio for the Arts, 149
Latham, Jean Lee, 29
Laughlin china, 120
Laurel Creek covered bridge, 107
Laurel Creek Winery, 131
Laurita, Joseph, 87
Layland, 80
Leatherbark Creek, 70
Lee, Henry (Light Horse Harry), 135
Lee, Robert E., 13, 15, 20, 78, 83, 103, 135, 137

Lee's White Sulphur Springs, 135
Leewood, 37
Left Hand, 60
Leon, 57
Leroy, 57
Lester, 57
Letter Gap, 60
Lewisburg, 47, 50, 56, 64, 65, 89, 98, 103, 113, 131, 132, 140, 148
Lewis County, 20, 51, 60, 61
Libbey-Owens, 35
Liberty, 131
Lilly Brothers, 22
Lillydale, 107
Lima, 61
Lincoln, Abraham, 16, 53
Lincoln County, 51, 53, 59, 61
Lindberg, Christian, 147
Lindside, 23, 88
liquor consumption, WV rank, 98
Little Beaver State Park, 74
Little Kanawha River, 102, 167, 168
Lochgelly, 81
Locust Creek, 107
Locus Creek covered bridge, 107
Logan, 25, 50, 73, 87, 140, 153, 162
Logan (Talgayeeta), 17, 68
Logan Banner, The, 140
Logan County, 50, 54, 57, 59, 68, 86
logging industry, 122
London, 61
"Lonesome 7-7203," 21
Long Branch Colliery, 81
Looneyville, 60
Lord, Suzanne, 112
Los Angeles Lakers, 33
Lost City, 134
Lost Creek, 74
Lost River State Park, 73, 135
Lost World Caverns, 103
"Love at the Five and Dime," 22
lowest point in WV, 98
lowest temperature in WV, 98
lumber towns, 122
Lunice Creek, 64
Lyle, Sparky, 155

ND # INDEX • 183

McArtor, Michael, 147
McCarthy, Joseph, 83
McCausland, John, 20
McClellan, George B., 78, 79
McColley, Connie and Tom, 24
MacCorkle, William A., 45, 117
McCoy, Charlie, 21
McCoy, "Old Ran'l," 83
McDowell County, 50, 56, 57, 58, 59, 60, 62, 68, 81, 124
Machine Dreams, 28, 143
McKay, John, 34
McKechnie, Bill, 152
McKenna, Colleen, 29
McMechen, 40
McVey, Mark, 147
Mad Butcher of West Virginia, 40
Madison, 51, 60
Maillard, Keith, 28, 143
Mail Pouch tobacco, 120
Main Bathhouse, Berkeley Springs, 71
Main Dining Room, The Greenbrier, 130
Malden, 15, 113, 122
Man, 59
Mannington, 153
Manson, Charles, 40
Maphis, 161
Marchetti, Gino, 32, 156, 157
Marie, 57
Marion County, 50, 55, 80, 81
Marland, William C., 47
Marlin's Bottom, 64
Marlinton, 52, 60, 64, 72, 73, 74, 76, 88, 100, 116
Marsh, Carole, 29
Marshall, George Preston, 157
Marshall, Peter, 25
Marshall County, 50, 55, 80
Marshall University, 30, 41, 85, 156
Martens, William F., 112
Martin, 57
Martinsburg, 15, 16, 29, 42, 43, 50, 55, 88, 94, 98, 111, 120, 129, 136, 140, 142, 149, 152
Mason County, 20, 35, 51, 53, 57, 59

Matala, Chuck, 24
Mate Creek, 47
Matewan, 38, 86-87, 142
Matewan (movie), 142
Matewan Massacre, 86-87
Mathews, Henry M., 45
Mathias, 73
Mattea, Kathy, 22
May, 59
Mays, Alvoid, 158
Mazeroski, Bill, 32
Meadow River, 108, 164
Meadows, Clarence W., 47
Meathouse Fork, 167
Mecklenburg, 64
Melissa, 57
Mercer County, 50, 55, 58, 59, 61, 62, 65
"Message to Garcia, A," 19
Methodist Protestant Church, first, 94
Metzger, Jon, 112
Mid-Atlantic Glass Factory, 126
Middle Atlantic League, 153
Middlebourne, 52
"Midnight Special," 21
Mill Creek, 67
Miller, Arnold Ray, 37, 38
Milton, 57, 105, 125
Mineral County, 16, 33, 42, 51
Mineral Daily News Tribune, Keyser, 140
Mingo, 95
Mingo (Native American), 17, 54, 68
Mingo County, 51, 57, 59, 62, 86
Mingo Oak, 95
"Mirror Lake," 103
"Miss Otis Regrets," 19
Mitchell, Paul, 161
Mitchum, Robert, 27
Moatsville, 24
Mobil Travel Guide, 100, 116, 130, 136, 137
Mohrman, Lou Ann, 24
Mole Hill, 47, 64
Moncover Lake State Park, 74
Monongah, 80, 81

Monongahela, The (railroad), 121
Monongahela National Forest, 76, 88
Monongahela River, 85, 102
Monongalia County, 45, 50, 55, 80, 87
Monroe, James, 53, 134
Monroe County, 20, 51, 53, 62, 65
Montcoal, 58
Montgomery, 153
moonshiners, 103
Moore, Arch A., Jr., 48
Moore, Sara Jane, 40
Moorefield, 51, 131
Morgan, Ephraim F., 17, 47, 112
Morgan County, 51, 108, 168
Morgantown, 24, 25, 29, 43, 50, 55, 67, 87, 100, 102, 106, 115, 120 131, 136, 140, 149, 156, 157
Morning Journal, The, Martinsburg, 140
Morris Harvey College, 30
Morrow, Anne (Lindbergh), 41
Morrow, Dwight, 41, 42
Morton, Levi P., 134
Moscow, 61
Mother Jones, 149
Mother's Day, first, 95, 114
Mott, Charles T., 112
Mott, Lou, 161
Moundsville, 27, 48, 50, 55, 75, 88, 95, 140, 145
Moundsville Daily Echo, 140
Mountain, 64
Mountain Heritage Arts & Crafts Festival, 91
Mountain House, 135
Mountain Stage, 117
Mountain State Art and Craft Fair, 92
Mountain State Forest Festival, 90
Mountain State League, 153
Mount Alto, 62
Mount Carbon, 62
Mount Clare, 62
Mount Gay, 62
Mount Hope, 62
Mount Liberty, 62

Mount Lookout, 62
Mount Nebo, 62
Mount Olive, 62
Mount Storm, 62
Mount Tabor, 62
Mount Vernon, 62
Mount Zion, 62
Mud, 59
Mud River, 105
Mud River covered bridge, 105
Mullens, 73, 161
Murray, Eddie, 154
Musial, Stan, 153
muskellunge, fishing record, 167
mussel, 110
Myers, Walter Dean, 29
My Father's Workshop, 23
"My Heart Keeps Crying," 21
Myra, 15
Myrtle, 57

Nat, 59
National Radio Astronomy Observatory, 71, 93, 100
National Steel Corp., 36
Native American population, WV rank, 98
Natural Heritage System, 108
Neal, 57
Neale, Earle (Greasy), 34, 157
Neal's Station, 64
Neely, Matthew M., 47
Never Say Never Again, 26
New Cumberland, 50, 64
Newell, 120
New England Fuel and Transportation Company, 80
New England Opera Theater, 23
New Era, 60
New Manchester, 74
New Martinsville, 51, 125, 162
Newport, Anne (Royall), 15
New River, 49, 69, 70, 72, 84, 102, 164, 167
New River Collieries Company, 80
New River Gorge, 70, 108, 164

New River Gorge Bridge, 90, 96, 104
New River Gorge National River, 75, 96
New River Park, 118
New Vrindaban, 89
New York Central, 121
New York Giants, 32
New York Stock Exchange, 37
New York Times, The, 80, 81, 84, 87
New York Times Book Review, 144
Nicholas County, 51, 54, 57, 59, 76
Nicklaus, Jack, 138
Night of the Hunter, The, 27, 30, 143
Nitro, 32, 67, 163
Norfolk and Western Railway, 121, 123
Norfolk Southern, 121, 123
North Bend State Park, 74
North Branch, Potomac River, 102
North Caperton, 70
Northern flying squirrel, 110
Northern pike, fishing record, 167
Northfork, 29
North Fork, South Branch, Potomac River, 167
Nugent, Tom, 149
Nuttalburg, 70
Nutter Fort, 131

Oak Hill, 21, 40, 83
Odd, 59
Odessa, 61
Oglebay Resort Park, 72, 99
Oglebay's Wilson Lodge, 136
Ohio County, 20, 50, 52, 55
Ohio-Pennsylvania League, 153
Ohio River, 17, 63, 84, 85, 99, 102, 104, 167, 168
Ohio River Valley, 145
O'Hurley's General Store, 127
Oka, 59
Old Bethany Meeting House, 113
Old Harmony Church, 94
Old Main, Bethany College, 115
Old Opera House, 149
Old Rehoboth Church, 114

Old Stone Presbyterian Church, 65, 113
"Old Sweet," 134
"Old White," 137
Oliverio's, 132
Ona, 59
One Flew over the Cuckoo's Nest, 26
Omar, 57
Opequon, Battle of, 20
"Orange Blossom Special," 21
Organ Cave, 103
Orr, 59
Ottawa, 61
Owens, Michael, 35

paddleboating, 166
paddlefish, fishing record, 168
Paddytown, 64
Paden, James R., 24
Paden City, 24
P. A. Denny (sternwheeler), 89
Paint Creek, 86
Palermo, 61
Pancake, Breece D'J, 145
Panther, 76
Panther State Forest, 76
Parcoal, 58
Parkersburg, 14, 25, 28, 34, 35, 37, 39, 45, 50, 55, 64, 69, 74, 84, 87, 88, 116, 120, 137, 140, 141, 157
Parkersburg News, The, 140, 141
Parkersburg Sentinel, The, 140, 141
Parsons, 52, 120
Patteson, Okey L., 47
Patton, George Smith, 111
Pauley, Kim, 147
People magazine, 22
Pearl S. Buck Birthplace Museum, 16, 118
Pearsall's Flats, 64
Pegram, John, 78
Pence Springs, 116, 130, 133
Pence Springs Hotel, 116, 134
Pendleton County, 52, 76, 98, 103, 126
peregrine falcon, 109

Personal Rapid Transit (PRT), 100, 115
Petersburg, 51, 56, 64
Peterstown, 96
"Phantom 309," 21
Philippi, 51, 64, 94, 105
Philippi, Battle of, 78, 79, 94
Philippi covered bridge, 77, 105
Phillips, Jayne Anne, 28, 143
Phillips Sheet & Tin Plate Co., 36
Pickens Bottom, 64
pickerel, fishing record, 167
Pickle Street, 60
Piedmont, 22, 41, 153
Pigeon Creek Hollow, 88
pike, Northern, fishing record, 167
Pilgrim Glass Corporation, 126
Pine Creek, 54
Pine Grove, 161
Pineville, 51, 60, 161
pink mucket pearly mussel, 110
Pinnacle Rock State Park, 74
Pipestem, 72, 73, 136
Pipestem Resort State Park, 72, 73, 136, 166
Pleasants County, 52, 61
Poca, 161, 163
Pocahontas County, 52, 54, 59, 60, 62, 70, 76, 88, 98
Pocahontas County Tourist Commission, 116
Poe, Edgar Allan, 30
Point Pleasant, 31, 51, 75, 85, 94, 104, 117, 122, 140
Point Pleasant, Battle of, 18, 94
Point Pleasant Battle Monument, 75
Point Pleasant Register, 140
Popovich, Paul, 32, 161, 162
Port Amherst, 96
Porter, Cole, 19
Porters Creek, 54
Post, Melville Davisson, 30, 31, 144
Potomac Highland Winery, 131
Potomac River, 14, 66, 94, 102, 131

Potomac State College, 42
Powell, Boog, 154
Powers, Harry F., 39
Prather, Charles, 63
Preston County, 51, 59, 67, 76
Pricketts Fort State Park, 75
Princeton, 32, 50, 55, 160, 161
Princeton Reds, 151
Pro Football Hall of Fame, 156-57
Prosperity, 62
Prudence, 62
Pudd'nhead Wilson, 142
Purgitsville, 131
Putnam County, 41, 50, 53, 55, 57, 62, 67

Queen Anne's lace, 108
Queen Victoria, 70
Quiet Dell, 40
quilting, 24
Quinwood, 56

railroad flatbed car, world's largest, 96
Rainbow Family murders, 88
Rainelle, 122
Raleigh County, 50, 55, 57, 58, 59, 61, 62, 68, 80
ramps, 90-91
Randolph County, 51, 52, 54, 55, 57, 58, 59, 65, 76, 95, 167
Rangoon, 61
Ransom, 56
Rapler, Melody, 147
Rathbone, Monroe J., 37
R. D. Bailey Lake, 107, 167
Rebels & Redcoats Tavern, 130
Reckless, 142
Red House Farms, 67
Redman, Don, 22
Red River, 25
Red Sulphur Springs, 134
Reed, Simpson, Thatcher and Barnum, NY, 41
Reedy, 37
Register-Herald, The, Beckley, 140

INDEX • 187

Reno, Jesse, 20
retail sales, WV rank, 98
Retreat at Buffalo Run, 129
Retton, Mary Lou, 33
Reuther, Walter, 37
Revolutionary War, 94
Reynolds, J. J., 78
Rhododendron Art and Craft Festival, 91
Rice, Otis, K., 150
Rich Mountain, Battle of, 78
Richwood, 18, 64, 90, 96, 122, 146
ringpink, 110
Ripkin, Bill, 154
Ripkin, Cal, Jr., 154
Ripley, 51, 60, 92
Ritchie County, 20, 51, 57, 59, 61, 64
Riverside Inn, 130
Riverton, 103
Roadside Hollywood, 142
Roane County, 51, 57, 59, 60, 61
Roanoke, 73
Robert F. Pliska Winery, 131
Robinson, Wil, 160
Rockefeller, John D. IV (Jay), 48
Rockne, Knute, 122
Rodgers, Ira Errett, 158
Roman Bath House, Berkeley Springs, 71
Rome, Italy, 19
Romney, 45, 51, 64, 129, 131, 161
Ronceverte, 103, 140
Roosevelt, Eleanor, 67, 70
Roosevelt, Franklin D., 67, 70
Rosecrans, William S., 78
Ross, Diana, 18
Rowan, Andrew S., 18, 19, 134
Royal Family of Broadway, The, 25
Royall, Anne, 15
Royall, William, 15
Rumsey, James, 14, 94
running buffalo clover, 108
rural free delivery of mail, first, 94
Rylant, Cynthia, 30

St. Albans, 55, 130

St. Denis, Charles, 89
St. John's Church, 105
St. Mary's, 52, 64, 104
sales tax, first, 95
saltpetre, 103
salt springs, 122
Salt Sulphur Springs, 106, 134
Sam Black Church, 60
Santiago, 61
Sarandon, Chris, 26
sauger, fishing record, 168
Sayles, John, 38, 142
Schneider's Winery, 131
Schwartz, Sergio, 147
Scott Depot, 126
Secoal, 58
Seneca Caverns, 103
Seneca Indians, 103
Seneca Rocks, 103, 126
Seneca State Forest, 76
Separate Peace, A, 27
Seth, 162
Settle, Mary Lee, 27
Sewell, 69-70
Shakur, Assata, 100
shale barren rockcress, 108
Shanghai, 61
Sharp's Country Store, 127
Shawnee (Native Americans), 18
Sheets, Larry, 154
Shenandoah River, 164
Shepherd College, 66, 115
Shepherdstown, 14, 64, 66, 94, 115, 116, 127, 131
Sheraton Lakeview Resort and Conference Center, 136
Sherman High School, Seth, 162
Sherrard High School, Wheeling, 161
Shinnston, 34, 84, 157
Silver Bridge, 85, 104
Simms & McNabb Brewery, 69
Simpson Thatcher and Bartlett, 44
Sinclair, Harry, 36
Sinclair Oil and Refining Corp., 36
Sistersville, 64, 161, 163
skipjack, fishing record, 168

ski resorts, 165
Skygusty, 62
Slatyfork, 127, 129, 165
Sleep Creek, 168
Sleepy Creek, 108
Sleepy Creek Lake, 167
"Slowpoke," 21
Smith, Ada Beatrice Queen Victoria Louise Virginia, 19
Smith, A. P. and E. P., 105
Smith, Hulett C., 16, 47
Smith, John, 54
Smithers, 32, 156, 157
Smoke Hole Caverns, 103
smoking, prevalence of in WV, 97
Smucker, Anna, 29
Snead, Sam, 138
Snowshoe/Silver Creek, 71, 127, 165
soda fountain, first
Sophia, 42
South Branch, Potomac River, 102, 164, 167, 168
South Branch Valley Rail, 121
South Charleston, 55, 161
Southern Airways crash, 85
South Fork, Hughes River, 167
South Mountain, Battle of, 20
Sovine, Red, 21
Space Apart, A, 28
Spencer, 51, 60, 64, 161
Spruce, 70
Spruce Knob, 98
Staggers, Harley O., Sr., 42
Standard Oil Co., 35, 37
Star City, 125
Starr, Ringo, 26
State Archives Library, 117
State Capitol, 46, 91, 99, 112
State Fair of West Virginia, 89
State Museum, Charleston, 117
State Theater, Charleston, 117
Statler, Ellsworth, 35-36
steamboat, invention of, 94
Steber, Eleanor, 23
Stephen, Adam, 111

Sterling faucets, 120
Sternwheel Regatta Festival, 89-90
Stevenson, William E., 45
Stoco High School, Coal City, 161
Stonecoal, 58
Stonecoal Lake, 168
Stonewall Jackson Heritage Art and Craft Jubilee, 92
Stonewall Jackson High School, 40
Stonewall Jackson Lake, 107
Stonewall Jackson Lake State Park, 73
Stoney Creek, 168
Stories of Breece D'J Pancake, The, 145
Storming Heaven, 28, 139, 144
Stotesbury, 42
Stout, Rex, 138
Stranger in Town, A, 26
Strauss, Lewis L., 44
strike, first nationwide, 94
Stuart, J. E. B., 83
Stuart mine, 81
sturgeon, fishing record, 168
Stydahar, Joe, 157
Suit, Samuel Taylor, 112
Summers County, 51, 57, 59
Summersville, 16, 51, 75, 131
Summersville Lake, 107
Sunrise Museum, 117
Suter, John F., 30-31
Sutton, 23, 24, 51, 149
Sutton Lake, 107
Sweet Dreams, 142
Sweet Springs, 134
swimming, WV rank, 97
Swisher, Jeff, 161, 163
Switchback, 81
sycamore, 95

"Take an Old Cold Tater," 21
"Take Me Home, Country Roads," 141
Talcott, 19
Talgayeeta (Logan), 17
Talley, Darryl, 158
Tams, 68

INDEX • 189

Tanners Crossroads, 64
Tariff, 60
Tate, Sharon, 40
Tau Kappa Epsilon, 88
Taylor, Edward, 88
Taylor, Jerry, 69
Taylor County, 51, 59, 61
Teapot Dome scandal, 36
"Teardrops on Your Letter," 21
Teays Valley, 55
"Teddy Bear," 21
tennis, WV rank, 97
Tentchurch Vineyard, 131
Thackston, Pete, 163
Theatre West Virginia, 148
Their Pilgrimage, 137
"This Is My West Virginia," 141
Thomas Shepherd Inn, 129
Thompson, Carlene, 31
Thorn, Rod, 32, 160, 161
Three Forks, 85
Three's Company, 26
Thunderbolt Express to Splashdown, 99
Thurmond, 49, 69, 142
Tiffany's Continental Key Club, 130
tiger musky, fishing record, 168
Timberline, 165
Times-West Virginian, Fairmont, 140
"Today I Started Loving You Again," 21
Tomlinson Run State Park, 74
Too Many Cooks, 138
Torn, Rip, 26
Tornado, 62
tornado of 1944, 84
tourist homes, 128
Townsend's big-eared bat, 109
train, longest freight, 96
Trans Allegheny Books, 116
"Trilobites," 145
Tri-State Airport, Huntington, 85
Tri-State League, 152
trout, fishing records, 168
Truman, Harry S, 44
Trumpet Unblown, The, 27
trust (in restraint of trade), 94

tuberculed-blossom pearly mussel, 110
Tucker County, 52, 57, 59, 76
Tug Fork, Big Sandy River, 60, 102
Tug Valley, 83
Tug Valley Chamber of Commerce, 68
Tunnel monitored by TV, first, 95
Tuskegee Institute, AL, 15
Twain, Mark, 142
Twelve Tales of Suspense and the Supernatural, 145
Twilight, 60
Twin Falls Resort State Park, 73
Tygart Lake, 107, 167, 168
Tygart Lake State Park, 74
Tygart River, *see* Tygart Valley River
Tygart Valley, 163
Tygart Valley Homesteads, 67
Tygart Valley River, 77, 102, 105, 164, 167
Tyler, Anne, 143
Tyler, John, 137
Tyler County, 52, 53, 57, 61, 96

Uncle Abner, 30
Uncle Abner, Master of Mysteries, 144
Underwood, Cecil H., 47, 48
Uneeda, 60
unemployment, teenage, in WV, 97
Union, 51, 65, 114
Union Carbide, 84, 120
Union Flint Glass Co., 35
United Automobile Workers (UAW), 37
United Methodist Church, 115
United Mine Workers of America (UMWA), 37, 38, 86, 87
Upshur County, 51, 59
Upshur County High School, 29
U.S. Fish and Wildlife Service, 109

Valley Falls State Park, 74
Valley Head, 21
Van Brocklin, Norm, 34
Van Buren, Martin, 134
Vance, Cyrus, 44

Van Damme, Andre, 147
Van Hook, Beverly, 29
Van Swearingen, Marmaduke (Blue Jacket), 18
Victoria, Queen, 70
videotaped evidence, first court to admit, 95
Vienna, 55, 61
Virginia big-eared bat, 109
Virginian, The (railroad), 121
Virginia Reels, 27
Virginia spiraea, 108
Virginia Valley League, 153
Volcano, 62, 69

Wakefield, Andy, 163
Walker, Fulton, 158
walking for exercise, WV rank, 97
Wallace, John, 39
walleye, fishing record, 168
"warden's rat," Moundsville, 88
Ware, Clyde, 27
Warm Springs, 134
Warner, Charles Dudley, 137
Warner, Curt, 32, 161
Washington, Booker T., 15, 113
Washington, Charles, 63, 66
Washington, George, 14, 63, 66, 133, 135
Washington and Lee University, 42, 43
Washington family, 114
Washington Irving High School, Clarksburg, 162
Watoga State Park, 73
Watson, Clarence W., 36
Watters Smith Memorial State Park, 74
Wayne, 50
Wayne, (Mad) Anthony, 18
Wayne County, 50, 57, 60
Waynesburg College, 34
Way You Look Tonight, The, 31
Weatherford, Teddy, 22
Weavers of Wood, 24
Webster, Daniel, 53, 54
Webster County, 51, 53, 54, 58, 76, 108

Webster Springs, 51, 64, 95
Wedding, A, 25
Weigen, Dick, 132
Weikel, Oscar, 105
Weikel, Ray, 105
Weir, Ernest, 36
Weir High School, 161
Weirton, 36, 55, 104, 140, 142
Weirton Daily Times, 140
Weirton Steel Co., 36, 119, 120
Welch, 50, 60, 140, 153, 159
Welch Daily News, The, 140
Wellington, 61
Wells, Alexander, 63
Wells, Kevin, 161
Wellsburg, 32, 51, 52, 63, 120, 125
Wesley Chapel, 115
West, Jerry, 33, 159, 160
Western Maryland (railroad), 121
Western Pennsylvania League, 153
West Fork River, 80, 85, 102
West Liberty, 56
Weston, 15, 51, 60, 64, 92
West Union, 52
Westvaco Corp., 123
West Virginia: A Guide to the Mountain State, 150
West Virginia: A History, 150
West Virginia: A History for Beginners, 150
West Virginia Advocate, 89
West Virginia Daily News, Lewisburg, Ronceverte, White Sulphur Springs, 140
West Virginia Department of Education and the Arts, 145, 146
West Virginia Division of Natural Resources, 145
West Virginia Division of Tourism & Parks, 164
West Virginia Hillbilly, The, 123, 146
"West Virginia Hills, The" 141
West Virginia History, 146
West Virginia League, 153
"West Virginia, My Home Sweet Home," 141

INDEX • 191

West Virginia Northern (railroad), 121
West Virginia One-Day Trip Book The, 112, 150
West Virginia Penitentiary, 88
West Virginia State Farm Museum, 117
West Virginia Symphony Orchestra, 147
West Virginia University, 29, 32, 33, 43, 44, 100, 115, 149, 156, 157, 158, 159-60
West Virginia Wesleyan College, 34, 115, 156, 157
West-Whitehill Winery, 131
Wetzel County, 51, 59
Wever-Werner-Atkins, 113
Wheeling, 17, 18, 22, 23, 25, 26, 28, 32, 35, 36, 37, 50, 55, 72, 83, 84, 94, 99, 120, 129, 130, 136, 140, 141, 147, 152
Wheeling News-Register, 140, 141
Wheeling Steel Company, 37, 80
Wheeling steel pails, 120
Wheeling suspension bridge, 104
When I Was Young in the Mountains, 30
"Where the Woodbine Twineth," 145
White, Albert B., 45
White Grass, 165
white oak, oldest, 95
White Sulphur Springs, 60, 65, 100, 133, 134, 135, 137, 138, 140
whitewater rafting, 164
Whittaker Station, 70
Widen, 68, 162
Wilcoe, 68
"Wild Cave Adventures," 103
Wildlife Resources Section, 110
Williams, Hank, 83
Williams, John Alexander, 105, 150
Williams, Ron, 161
Williamson, 51, 58, 60, 68, 83, 140, 153
Williamson Daily News, 140
Williams River, 102
Williamstown, 112, 125

Willis, Meredith Sue, 28
Willow Island, 85
Wilson, Emanuel W., 45
Wilson, Hack, 152
Wilson, William L., 43
Wilson, Woodrow, 42, 43, 137
Wilson-Kelly, Becky, 29
Winchester, VA, 142
Winchester & Western (railroad), 121
Winding Gulf, 68
Windy, 62
Winfield, 50, 56
Winifrede (railroad), 121
WinterPlace, 165
Wirt County, 52, 57, 62
Wobbly Tooth, The, 29
Wolf Pen, 60
Wonderful West Virginia, 70, 145
Wood County, 39, 50, 53, 55, 61, 62, 69
Woods Resort & Conference Center, The, 136
Wood Works, 24
Worby, Rachael, 147
Workman, Mark, 159
Worthington, Craig, 154
WPA writers, 122, 150
Wyco, 26
Wyoming, 32
Wyoming County, 51, 57, 58, 59, 60, 62, 68

Yeager, Charles (Chuck) 15, 95
Yellow Brick Bank, 116
yellow perch, fishing record, 167
Yesterdays, Ltd., 129
Yost, Fielding Harris (Hurry Up), 33
Young Landlords, The, 30
Youth Museum of Southern West Virginia, 118

Zane, Ebenezer, 17
Zane, Elizabeth (Betty), 17
"Zeke from Cabin Creek," 33
Ziggletown, 64
Zion Episcopal Church, 114

About the Authors

Gerald Tomlinson, writer, editor, and publisher, is the author of *On a Field of Black*, a mystery novel set in the anthracite region of Pennsylvania. The author of more than twenty mystery short stories, he has written, most recently, *Murdered in Jersey* and, with Ronald A. Mayer, *The New Jersey Book of Lists*. A native of Elmira, New York, he graduated from Marietta College and now lives in Lake Hopatcong, New Jersey, with his wife Alexis. For more than twenty years he held editorial and executive positions in book publishing.

Richard C. Weigen has spent much of his working life traveling in West Virginia, selecting sites for gas stations and convenience stores. A native of Long Island, New York, he now resides with his wife Bonnie in Sutton, West Virginia, where he is president of Strictly Business, Inc., a bookstore. He owns Corporate Book Resources, an *Inc 500* company that supplies books to corporations, governments, and other organizations worldwide. The rest of the time he does research, reading, and real estate consulting.